Rugby Stories for Girls

Volume 1

By Tanya P. Lovejoy

Contents

Introduction	**6**
1. The Magic Rugby Boots	**10**
○ Part One	10
○ Part Two	15
○ Part Three	24
○ Part Four	31
○ Part Five	36
○ Part Six	41
2. Try for the Stars	**48**
○ Part One	48
○ Part Two	53
○ Part Three	59
○ Part Four	65
○ Part Five	75
○ Part Six	82

3. Under the Rugby Rainbow   **90**

- Part One   90
- Part Two   99
- Part Three   108
- Part Four   115
- Part Five   121
- Part Six   129

4. The Unstoppable Scrum   **137**

- Part One   137
- Part Two   141
- Part Three   146
- Part Four   152
- Part Five   160
- Part Six   169

5. **The International Exchange** **177**
    - Part One 177
    - Part Two 182
    - Part Three 187
    - Part Four 192
    - Part Five 197
    - Part Six 202

Thank-You From The Author **210**

Introduction

Dear Readers,

Firstly, a heartfelt thank you for choosing **Rugby Stories for Girls - Volume 1!**

As you journey through the pages, I'm thrilled to share in the exciting world of rugby with you. I hope the tales within this book bring as much joy to you as they did to me while writing.

Writing is a passion of mine and I aspire to continue crafting stories that resonate with young hearts, but it's very hard to compete against the big publishing houses.

However, your reviews can make the difference.

Your reviews empower me to keep writing, and I genuinely treasure and delight in each one I read.

So, with this in mind, **it would mean the world to me if you could share your thoughts in an Amazon review.**

Thank you for being an integral part of my writing adventure.

Warm regards,

Tanya

The Magic Rugby Boots

Part 1

In the picturesque town of Oakridge, nestled amidst the rolling hills of the English countryside, there lived a young girl named Ellie. With her vibrant spirit and fiery red hair, Ellie was a force of nature in her own right. At the tender age of ten, she was already well-known for her love of rugby, a sport that was more like a passion to her.

Ellie had grown up watching her father play rugby for the local club, the Oakridge Otters. From the moment she could walk, she was chasing after rugby balls, practicing tackles on imaginary opponents, and even attempting to kick conversions in the family garden. She was determined to follow in her father's footsteps and make a name for herself on the rugby field.

Every afternoon after school, Ellie could be found at Oakridge Primary School's rugby pitch, where she trained with the school's girls' rugby team. She loved every moment of it, from the rush of sprinting down the field with the ball to the camaraderie she shared with her teammates. But despite her boundless enthusiasm, Ellie faced a challenge that often left her feeling disheartened.

You see, Ellie was one of the smallest and youngest players on the team. While she possessed the heart of a lion and a determination that could move mountains, she lacked the physical size and strength of some of her teammates. As a result, she often struggled to keep up with them during practice.

One sunny afternoon, as Ellie huffed and puffed her way through yet another tackling drill, her friend and teammate, Lucy, patted her on the back. "You did great, Ellie!"

Ellie managed a tired smile. "Thanks, Lucy, but I wish I could be faster and stronger. I want to be a star player like Dad!"

Lucy, who had known Ellie for as long as she could remember, understood her friend's determination. "You'll get there, Ellie. Just keep practicing, and you'll surprise everyone one day."

Despite Lucy's encouraging words, Ellie couldn't help but feel a pang of frustration. She yearned to make her mark on the rugby field, to be a standout player like her father. But how could she achieve that when she often found herself outmuscled and outrun by her older and larger teammates?

One day, after yet another practice that left her feeling inadequate, Ellie decided to take a different route home. She wanted some time alone to clear her head and think about her future in rugby. She strolled through the charming streets of Oakridge, her rugby boots slung over her shoulder, lost in thought.

As she meandered past the town square, Ellie's eyes caught a glimpse of something unusual in the window of a small sports shop named "Sporting Dreams." The shop was known for its eclectic collection of sporting equipment, and its proprietor, Mr. Higgins, had a reputation for keeping rare and vintage items in stock.

Curiosity piqued, Ellie stepped into the shop, the bell above the door tinkling softly. Sporting Dreams was a treasure trove of sports memorabilia, from ancient cricket bats to vintage football jerseys. But what caught Ellie's eye that day was a pair of rugby boots, unlike any she had ever seen before.

Tucked away in a dusty corner of the shop, these boots looked both ancient and mystical. They were made of worn brown leather, with faded laces and sturdy metal studs on the soles. The boots seemed to whisper tales of legendary players and epic matches from days gone by.

Ellie couldn't resist examining them closer. She carefully picked up one of the boots and marveled at its craftsmanship. "They must be really old," she thought aloud.

Mr. Higgins, a stout man with a white beard and twinkling eyes, appeared from behind a shelf of cricket bats. "Ah, you've got a keen eye, young miss. Those boots have a history, they do."

Ellie looked at Mr. Higgins, her curiosity piqued. "What kind of history?"

Mr. Higgins leaned in conspiratorially. "Well, legend has it that those boots once belonged to a rugby player who was known for his incredible speed and accuracy. They say he could score a try from anywhere on the field."

Ellie's eyes widened. She had heard stories of legendary rugby players, but this was something extraordinary. "Is that true?"

Mr. Higgins chuckled. "Who's to say, young miss? But I do know one thing – those boots have a touch of magic about them. If you put them on, you might just find yourself running faster and kicking straighter than you ever thought possible."

Ellie was intrigued, but she couldn't help but be skeptical. "Magic boots? Really?"

Mr. Higgins nodded solemnly. "Aye, you never know until you try them on. Sometimes, all it takes is a little magic to unlock your true potential."

As Ellie gazed at the boots, a spark of excitement ignited within her. The idea of owning boots that could make her a better rugby player was too enticing to resist. She knew she didn't have much money, but she had been saving her pocket money for a special occasion. This, she decided, was that occasion.

"How much are they?" she asked, her voice filled with determination.

Mr. Higgins named a price, and Ellie didn't hesitate. She counted out her hard-earned pocket money and handed it over to the shopkeeper. With a sense of anticipation, she carefully placed the magical-looking rugby boots into her bag and left the shop.

Little did Ellie know that those seemingly ordinary boots would soon lead her on an extraordinary journey, one filled with surprising twists, newfound abilities, and a lesson about the true magic of rugby. As she walked home that day, the weight of the boots in her bag felt like a promise of something incredible waiting to unfold.

Part 2

The days following Ellie's acquisition of the mysterious rugby boots were filled with a blend of curiosity and anticipation. She couldn't shake the feeling that she held something extraordinary in her hands. As she approached the rugby pitch for the next practice session, her heart raced with excitement.

Ellie had decided to keep her newfound boots a secret, at least for now. She wanted to see for herself if they truly possessed any magic before sharing her discovery with anyone else. Clutching the bag that contained the boots, she slipped onto the field, hoping that they would be the key to unlocking her full potential as a rugby player.

Coach Wilson, a stern but fair instructor, was leading the practice that day. Ellie joined the circle of her teammates as they prepared for another round of drills. She watched as the coach explained the exercise and the girls began to warm up.

The moment of truth had arrived. Ellie crouched down to tie her old, worn rugby boots – the ones she had been using for as long as she could remember. She hesitated for a moment, her hand hovering over the new boots in her bag. With a deep breath, she decided it was time to give them a try.

Carefully, she slid the ancient-looking boots onto her feet, marveling at how snugly they fit. They felt surprisingly comfortable, as if they had been custom-made for her. Ellie stood up, feeling an odd sense of excitement coursing through her.

As the practice commenced, something incredible happened. Ellie felt a rush of energy surging through her legs, as if she had been injected with newfound power. She sprinted faster than she had ever run before, leaving her teammates in the dust as she charged toward the try line.

With a burst of agility, she sidestepped an opponent and made a perfect pass to Lucy, who was waiting near the try line. Lucy caught the ball and scored effortlessly. The entire team stared in amazement, including Coach Wilson.

"Ellie, that was incredible!" Lucy exclaimed, panting with exertion.

Ellie could hardly believe it herself. It was as if the boots had transformed her into a rugby dynamo. She felt faster, more agile, and her kicks were incredibly accurate. She couldn't help but grin from ear to ear.

Coach Wilson approached Ellie with a raised eyebrow. "That was some impressive play, Ellie. It's like you've turned into a different player."

Ellie tried to hide her astonishment. "I guess I had a good day, Coach."

But as the practice continued, it became clear that Ellie's performance wasn't a one-time fluke. Time and time again, she sprinted past her opponents with ease, tackled with precision, and made passes that were pinpoint accurate. Her teammates watched in awe, and Coach Wilson couldn't contain her excitement.

"Ellie, I've never seen anything like this before! You're playing like a seasoned pro. Keep it up!"

Ellie felt a mixture of exhilaration and trepidation. The boots were indeed magical, there was no doubt about it. But what would happen if her secret were to be revealed? Would her teammates think she was cheating, or worse, that she wasn't the player they thought she was?

In the following weeks, Ellie's newfound abilities continued to amaze everyone. Her school's rugby team went from being an underdog to a formidable opponent. Victories piled up, and it wasn't long before they were considered a force to be reckoned with. Ellie had become the star player, the one who could turn the tide of a match with her incredible skills.

The news of Ellie's remarkable transformation spread like wildfire through the school and the town of Oakridge. She was no longer just a rugby enthusiast; she was a local legend in the making. Her family, especially her father, couldn't have been prouder of her accomplishments.

But as the weeks passed, something began to trouble Ellie. She couldn't shake the feeling that her success was solely due to the magic in the boots. She had always dreamed of becoming a great rugby player through hard work and dedication, but now it seemed like she was relying on an external source of power.

One evening, as she sat in her room, Ellie confided in her best friend, Mia. "Mia, there's something I haven't told anyone. It's about these boots." She reached under her bed and pulled out the ancient-looking rugby boots.

Mia's eyes widened as she examined the boots. "Wow, they look incredible! But what's the secret?"

Ellie hesitated before explaining, "They make me a better rugby player, Mia. I can run faster, kick more accurately, and tackle with precision. It's like magic."

Mia looked both amazed and concerned. "That sounds amazing, Ellie! But why haven't you told anyone?"

"I'm afraid, Mia," Ellie admitted. "Afraid that people will think I'm cheating, or that I'm not really as good as they think I am. I want to be a great rugby player because of my hard work and dedication, not because of these boots."

Mia nodded sympathetically. "I understand, Ellie. But maybe you can use the boots as a tool to become a better player, and then show everyone that your skills are your own, with or without them."

Ellie considered Mia's words. Maybe she could use the boots as a means to improve her skills further, and then prove to herself and others that she was a talented rugby player because of her dedication and effort, not just because of a pair of magical boots.

With renewed determination, Ellie decided to continue using the boots during practices and matches, but she also began to focus on honing her natural abilities. She spent hours practicing her passes, perfecting her kicks, and working on her fitness. She was determined to become the best rugby player she could be, with or without the boots' magic.

As the school rugby team prepared for an important match against their arch-rivals, Ellie faced a dilemma. Should she wear the boots and risk people thinking she was relying on them, or should she prove herself without their help?

The day of the match arrived, and Ellie stood on the sideline, torn between the magical boots in her bag and the desire to prove herself without them. Coach Wilson approached her, sensing her inner struggle.

"Ellie, I've seen your dedication and hard work in training. You have the potential to be a phenomenal rugby player. Use whatever you need to play your best today."

Ellie made a decision. She tied her old, worn rugby boots and left the magical ones in her bag. It was time to show everyone, including herself, what she was truly capable of.

The match was intense, with both teams giving their all. Ellie was a whirlwind of energy on the field, making tackles, setting up plays, and demonstrating her newfound skills. She felt a renewed sense of pride in her abilities, knowing that she was playing with her own strength and dedication.

As the match entered its final minutes, the score was tied, and both teams were locked in a fierce battle. Ellie's team had possession of the ball, and they needed a try to win. The pressure was on, and Ellie could feel her heart pounding in her chest.

With a burst of determination, Ellie led a brilliant attack down the field. She dodged opponents, made a clever pass to Mia, and then sprinted toward the try line. Mia caught the ball and drew the last defender, leaving Ellie with a clear path to victory.

But as Ellie approached the try line, she hesitated for a split second. The thought of using the magical boots to ensure her victory crossed her mind. However, in that moment of hesitation, she made a decision that would change everything.

Ellie took a deep breath, planted her feet firmly in the ground, and dove for the try line with all her might. She could feel the defender closing in, but she stretched out her arm, reaching for the line. The referee's whistle blew, and the crowd held its breath as Ellie touched the ball down just inches from the try line.

The stadium erupted in cheers as Ellie's team celebrated their hard-fought victory. Ellie had made the winning play with her own skill and determination, without relying on the magic of the boots.

Coach Wilson approached Ellie with a proud smile. "That was an incredible try, Ellie. You've proven to everyone, including yourself, that you're a remarkable rugby player because of your hard work and dedication."

Tears of joy filled Ellie's eyes as she realized the truth of Coach Wilson's words. The magic of the boots had given her a boost, but her true strength lay in her commitment to the game and the power of teamwork.

From that day forward, Ellie continued to wear the magical boots during practice, but she no longer relied on them during matches. She worked tirelessly to improve her skills and became a true leader on the team. She learned that while the boots had given her a taste of magic, the real magic of rugby was in the dedication, practice, and the unwavering support of her teammates.

As Ellie grew older and her rugby career advanced, she decided to pass on the magic boots to a younger player, just as Mr.

Higgins had suggested. She wanted to inspire the next generation to believe in themselves and the power of teamwork, rather than relying on magic.

The story of Ellie and her magic rugby boots became a legend in Oakridge, a tale that reminded everyone that true greatness could be achieved through hard work, dedication, and the belief in one's own abilities. And as Ellie continued to play and inspire others, she knew that the magic of rugby would always be a part of her, with or without the boots.

Part 3

As word spread about Ellie's extraordinary performance during that pivotal match, her reputation as a rugby prodigy skyrocketed. She was no longer just a young girl from a small town; she was becoming a local legend, a rising star in the world of rugby. The school hallways buzzed with excitement every time Ellie walked by, and her classmates couldn't help but admire her incredible talent.

Ellie, however, was grappling with a newfound challenge – fame. Everywhere she went, people wanted to talk to her about rugby. Parents and teachers praised her, while her classmates sought her advice on improving their game. It was flattering, but it also brought immense pressure.

One afternoon, as Ellie was heading to the school's rugby field for practice, she overheard a group of girls whispering excitedly nearby.

"Isn't that Ellie? The one who's like a rugby superstar now?" one girl said, her eyes wide with admiration.

"Yeah, I heard she's unbeatable with those magical boots," another girl added.

Ellie's heart sank at the mention of the "magical boots." She knew that her newfound abilities were due to the boots, but she also wanted to prove herself without relying on them. The pressure to maintain her superstar status was overwhelming.

As she joined her teammates on the field, Ellie noticed their expectant looks. They had come to rely on her skills to win matches, and they were counting on her to lead them to victory once again. Coach Wilson, however, seemed to sense Ellie's unease.

"Ellie, remember, you're part of a team. We win together and lose together. Don't put too much pressure on yourself," Coach Wilson reminded her.

Ellie nodded, trying to shake off the weight of expectation. She loved rugby, and she loved her team, but she couldn't help but wonder if she would ever be able to prove that she was more than just the girl with the magical boots.

As the weeks went by, Ellie's school rugby team continued to dominate their opponents. Her skills, coupled with the clever strategies Coach Wilson had developed, made them a formidable force on the field. Victories piled up, and Ellie's confidence soared.

But with each win, Ellie's reliance on the boots grew. She began to believe that her success was solely because of the magic in the boots, and that without them, she would be nothing more than an average player. The boots had become a crutch, and

Ellie couldn't help but feel that they were holding her back from reaching her full potential.

One evening, after a particularly grueling practice, Ellie sat in her room, staring at the boots. They lay on the floor, gleaming with an otherworldly aura. She couldn't deny their power, but she also knew that she needed to break free from their hold.

"I can't keep relying on you," Ellie whispered to the boots. "I want to be a great rugby player because of my own hard work and dedication."

Determined to prove herself, Ellie made a difficult decision. The next day, she left the boots at home and wore her old, worn rugby boots to practice. It was a bold move, one that filled her with anxiety and uncertainty. Would she be able to perform without the boots' magic?

As she joined her teammates on the field, Ellie felt a surge of nervousness. She was no longer the unstoppable force they had come to rely on. She was just Ellie, a girl who loved rugby and was determined to play her best.

The practice session was tough, and Ellie struggled to keep up with her teammates. She missed tackles, her passes were less accurate, and her kicks didn't have the same precision. The realization that she had become dependent on the boots hit her hard.

At the end of practice, Coach Wilson approached Ellie with a concerned look. "Ellie, is everything okay? You seemed a bit off today."

Ellie hesitated, unsure of how to explain. "I...I left my boots at home today, Coach. I wanted to see if I could still play without them."

Coach Wilson nodded thoughtfully. "That's a brave decision, Ellie. It's important to remember that your skills and talent are your own, with or without the boots. But if they help you, don't be afraid to use them."

Ellie appreciated her coach's understanding, but she knew that she needed to prove herself without relying on the boots. She spent the next few weeks practicing tirelessly, focusing on improving her skills, and regaining her confidence.

The day of the important match against their arch-rivals finally arrived. Ellie stood on the sideline, her heart pounding with nervous anticipation. She had chosen to wear her old boots once again, determined to show everyone, including herself, that she could be a great rugby player on her own merits.

The match was intense from the start. Both teams were evenly matched, and the competition was fierce. Ellie's teammates looked to her for leadership, but she knew that she had to prove herself without the boots' magic.

As the game progressed, Ellie made a series of crucial plays. She tackled opponents with precision, set up clever passes, and displayed her natural agility on the field. Her teammates rallied around her, and they fought hard for every inch of the field.

With just minutes left in the match, the score was tied. The tension was palpable, and Ellie could feel the weight of the moment. This was her chance to prove that she was more than just the girl with the magical boots.

As the opposing team launched a fierce attack, Ellie found herself in a one-on-one situation with the ball carrier. She braced herself for the collision, determined to make a clean tackle. With all her strength and skill, she brought the opponent down, preventing them from scoring.

The referee's whistle blew, signaling a turnover in possession. Ellie's teammates cheered her on, and she felt a surge of pride. She had made a crucial play, and it was all thanks to her own skill and determination.

The match continued, and as the clock ticked down, Ellie's team found themselves in a scoring position. With a series of quick passes and strategic moves, they worked their way toward the try line. Ellie knew that this was their moment.

With a burst of energy, she led the final charge, sprinting toward the try line with the ball in hand. The opposing team's defense closed in, but Ellie refused to let anything stand in her way. She dived for the try line, stretching out her arm with every ounce of strength she had left.

The referee's whistle blew, and the stadium erupted in cheers. Ellie had scored the winning try, securing their victory. Her teammates surrounded her, lifting her onto their shoulders in celebration.

Coach Wilson approached Ellie with a proud smile. "You did it, Ellie. You proved that you're a phenomenal rugby player because of your hard work and dedication, not just because of a pair of magical boots."

Tears of joy filled Ellie's eyes as she realized the truth of Coach Wilson's words. She had broken free from the hold of the magical boots and rediscovered her love for rugby. The real magic of the game was in her dedication, practice, and the unwavering support of her teammates.

From that day forward, Ellie continued to wear the magical boots during practices, but she no longer relied on them during matches. She had learned that while the boots had given her a taste of magic, the real magic of rugby was in the dedication, practice, and the belief in one's own abilities.

As Ellie grew older and her rugby career advanced, she decided to pass on the magic boots to a younger player, just as Mr. Higgins had suggested. She wanted to inspire the next generation to believe in themselves and the power of teamwork, rather than relying on magic.

The story of Ellie and her magic rugby boots became a legend in Oakridge, a tale that reminded everyone that true greatness could be achieved through hard work, dedication, and the belief in one's own abilities. And as Ellie continued to play and inspire others, she knew that the magic of rugby would always be a part of her, with or without the boots.

Part 4

The days grew shorter, and the chill of autumn hung in the air as Ellie and her rugby team continued to train and play matches. The Oakridge Owls, as they were known, were now a formidable force in the local rugby scene, and Ellie was at the heart of their success.

Despite her initial hesitance, Ellie had made the bold decision to leave her magic rugby boots at home during matches. She wanted to prove to herself and to everyone else that she could excel on the rugby field through her own skills, dedication, and teamwork.

Her teammates respected her choice and rallied around her. They saw the determination in her eyes and knew that she was not just the girl with the magical boots but a fierce competitor who could hold her own. The bonds of their team grew stronger with each practice and match.

One chilly Saturday morning, as Ellie laced up her old rugby boots in the locker room before a crucial match against their rivals, the Greenfield Griffins, she felt a mixture of excitement and nervousness. The Griffins were known for their tough, physical style of play, and the match promised to be a hard-fought battle.

Coach Wilson gathered the team in a pre-match huddle, her voice filled with confidence. "Remember, Owls, we're a team, and we're here to win together. Ellie has shown us that we don't need magic boots to be successful. Let's go out there, give it our all, and play like champions."

The Owls ran onto the pitch, and the crowd erupted in cheers. The match was intense from the start, with both teams giving their all. Ellie, determined to prove herself, tackled opponents with precision, made accurate passes, and showed her natural agility on the field. Her teammates matched her intensity, and they fought hard for every inch of the field.

As the match wore on, Ellie found herself in one challenging situation after another. She was often double-teamed by the Griffins, who were determined to shut her down. But Ellie refused to be intimidated. She relied on her training and her teammates, knowing that together, they could overcome any obstacle.

The score remained tied as the clock ticked down, and tension filled the air. With just minutes left in the match, the Owls found themselves deep in Griffin territory, with a prime opportunity to score. Ellie could feel the weight of the moment, and she knew that this was their chance.

With a burst of energy, Ellie led the final charge, sprinting toward the try line with the ball in hand. The Griffin's defense closed in, and Ellie could hear the shouts of her teammates urging her on. She could also hear the voice of doubt whispering in the back of her mind, tempting her to rely on the magical boots just this once.

But Ellie pushed those doubts aside. She knew that this was a test of her resolve and her commitment to the game. With every ounce of strength and determination, she dived for the try line, stretching out her arm with all her might.

The referee's whistle blew, and the stadium erupted in cheers. Ellie had scored the winning try, securing their victory. Her teammates surrounded her, lifting her onto their shoulders in celebration.

Coach Wilson approached Ellie with a proud smile. "You did it, Ellie. You proved that you're a phenomenal rugby player because of your hard work and dedication, not just because of a pair of magical boots."

Tears of joy filled Ellie's eyes as she realized the truth of Coach Wilson's words. She had broken free from the hold of the magical boots and rediscovered her love for rugby. The real magic of the game was in her dedication, practice, and the unwavering support of her teammates.

The days turned into weeks, and Ellie continued to wear her old rugby boots during matches. She had learned that while the magical boots had given her a taste of magic, the true power of rugby was in the belief in one's own abilities and the strength of teamwork.

One sunny afternoon, after a particularly satisfying victory, Ellie decided it was time to have a conversation with Mr. Higgins, the kindly sports shop owner who had sold her the magical boots. She wanted to thank him for introducing her to rugby and for the incredible journey she had embarked on.

As Ellie entered the small sports shop, she saw Mr. Higgins behind the counter, organizing a stack of rugby balls. He looked up and smiled warmly when he saw Ellie.

"Ellie! What brings you here today?" he asked.

"I wanted to talk to you about the magic rugby boots," Ellie replied.

Mr. Higgins nodded and motioned for her to sit on a nearby bench. "Ah, those boots have quite a story, don't they? How have they been treating you?"

Ellie smiled, thinking back on her journey. "They've been amazing, Mr. Higgins. They helped me discover my love for rugby, and I've had some incredible experiences. But I've also learned that the real magic of rugby is in hard work, dedication, and teamwork."

Mr. Higgins nodded thoughtfully. "You've learned a valuable lesson, Ellie. The boots can give you a boost, but it's your passion and commitment that make you a true rugby player. What are you thinking of doing with the boots now?"

Ellie hesitated for a moment before answering. "I want to pass them on to someone else, someone who needs a little boost to discover their own potential. Just like you did for me."

Mr. Higgins's eyes twinkled with understanding. "That's a wonderful idea, Ellie. I'm sure the boots will find their way to the right person. And who knows, maybe someday, you'll inspire them to believe in themselves, just like you did."

As Ellie left the sports shop that day, she felt a sense of closure and fulfillment. She had come full circle in her rugby journey, from a shy girl who stumbled upon a pair of magical boots to a confident player who understood the true meaning of the game.

The story of Ellie and her magic rugby boots became a legend in Oakridge, a tale that reminded everyone that true greatness could be achieved through hard work, dedication, and the belief in one's own abilities. And as Ellie continued to play and inspire others, she knew that the magic of rugby would always be a part of her, with or without the boots.

Part 5

After Ellie's triumphant match without the magic rugby boots, her confidence soared, and she felt a renewed sense of purpose. She had proven to herself and her teammates that her success on the rugby field was a result of her hard work, dedication, and the power of teamwork.

The Oakridge Owls, led by Ellie and their dedicated coach, Wilson, continued to dominate their opponents. Their clever strategies, precision passes, and relentless teamwork made them a formidable force in the local rugby scene. Victories piled up, and their reputation as a team that played with heart and skill grew.

But it wasn't just about winning for Ellie and her teammates. They had learned that rugby was more than just a game; it was a bond that connected them on and off the field. They shared victories, losses, and the countless hours of training that made them a tight-knit group.

As the rugby season progressed, the Owls faced tougher opponents, including teams from neighboring towns and cities. Each match was a test of their skills and their ability to work together as a team. Ellie, now playing without the magical boots, continued to shine as a leader on the field. She tackled opponents with precision, set up clever passes, and displayed her natural agility.

But it wasn't just Ellie who stood out. Her teammates had grown immensely as players and individuals. Emily, the scrappy forward, had become a master of lineouts and was known for her fearless tackles. Lily, the quick-witted scrum-half, could read the game like a book, setting up plays that left opponents bewildered. And Sarah, the powerful prop, was a force to be reckoned with in scrums and rucks.

The bond between Ellie and her teammates deepened as they faced challenges together. They celebrated victories with high-fives and cheers and offered support and encouragement during tough losses. The Owls were more than just a rugby team; they were a family.

One sunny Saturday morning, the Owls gathered for a match against a formidable opponent, the Riverdale Ravens. The Ravens were known for their physicality and aggressive style of play, and they were determined to break the Owls' winning streak.

The match was intense from the first whistle. The Ravens launched a relentless attack, pushing the Owls back with their sheer force. Ellie and her teammates were put to the test, and they responded with unwavering determination.

As the game progressed, it became clear that the Ravens were not going to give up easily. They were a formidable adversary, and they pushed the Owls to their limits. The score remained tied as the clock ticked down, and tension filled the air.

With just minutes left in the match, the Ravens had possession of the ball and were closing in on the Owls' try line. The Owls' defense held strong, but the Ravens were determined to break through.

Ellie, as the captain, rallied her teammates. "We've faced tough opponents before, and we've overcome every challenge together. Let's show them what the Owls are made of!"

Her teammates nodded in agreement, their determination matching Ellie's. They knew that this was a defining moment, a test of their resilience and teamwork.

As the Ravens launched a final assault, Ellie found herself in the midst of a scrum, fighting for control of the ball. She could feel the Ravens' relentless pressure, but she refused to give in. With her teammates by her side, they held their ground, and the Ravens were forced to make an error.

The referee's whistle blew, signaling a turnover in possession. The Owls had the ball, and they knew that this was their chance to secure victory. With a series of quick passes and strategic moves, they worked their way toward the Ravens' try line.

Ellie, once again, led the final charge. She sprinted toward the try line with the ball in hand, the Ravens' defense closing in. But

Ellie had learned that the real magic of rugby was in the belief in one's own abilities and the strength of teamwork.

With a burst of energy, she dived for the try line, stretching out her arm with all her might. The stadium erupted in cheers as the referee's whistle blew, confirming the try. The Owls had secured a hard-fought victory.

Ellie's teammates rushed to her, lifting her onto their shoulders in celebration. Coach Wilson beamed with pride as she watched her team's triumphant moment.

"You did it, Owls," Coach Wilson said. "You faced a tough opponent, and you proved that with hard work, dedication, and teamwork, you can overcome any challenge. This victory belongs to all of you."

As the Owls celebrated their victory, Ellie couldn't help but reflect on her journey. She had come a long way from the shy girl who had stumbled upon a pair of magical rugby boots. She had discovered the true magic of rugby – the power of teamwork, determination, and the belief in oneself.

The story of Ellie and her teammates became a source of inspiration for their small town of Oakridge. It was a reminder that true greatness could be achieved through hard work and unity. The Owls continued to play the game they loved, not as individuals with magical boots, but as a team that played with heart and soul.

And as Ellie looked at her teammates, their smiles reflecting the joy of their hard-earned victory, she knew that she had found her place in the world of rugby. The magic of the game was not in the boots; it was in the friendships, the challenges, and the victories that they shared as a team.

Part 6

The sun was beginning to set on a crisp autumn evening in Oakridge as the Oakridge Owls gathered on their home rugby pitch for their final match of the season. The stands were filled with enthusiastic supporters, including parents, friends, and even some of the younger rugby enthusiasts who looked up to the Owls as their heroes.

This was no ordinary match; it was the championship game against their arch-rivals, the Greenfield Griffins. The rivalry between the two teams was fierce, and this match was the culmination of a season filled with hard work, determination, and growth.

Ellie, now 12 years old, stood proudly as the captain of the Oakridge Owls. Her journey from a timid girl who stumbled upon a pair of magical rugby boots to a confident and skilled rugby player was nothing short of remarkable. She had learned that the real magic of rugby was not in the boots but in the dedication, practice, and the belief in one's own abilities.

As the team huddled together before the match, Coach Wilson spoke passionately, "This is it, Owls. The championship is within our grasp, but it won't be easy. We've come a long way, and we've proven that we're a team to be reckoned with. Let's go out there and show the world what the Owls are made of!"

The Owls ran onto the pitch to the deafening roar of the crowd. The Griffins were a formidable opponent, known for their physicality and aggressive style of play. The match promised to be a fierce battle, and the tension was palpable.

The first half of the match was a brutal contest of strength and strategy. Both teams fought fiercely for control of the ball, with tackles and scrums that left the players covered in mud. The score remained close, with neither team willing to give an inch.

Ellie, playing without the magical rugby boots, was a force to be reckoned with on the field. She tackled opponents with precision, made strategic passes, and used her natural agility to her advantage. Her teammates matched her intensity, and they fought hard for every inch of the field.

As the clock ticked down in the second half, the Owls found themselves in a challenging situation. The Griffins had possession of the ball and were advancing toward the Owls' try line. The pressure was immense, and Ellie could feel the weight of the moment.

With just minutes left in the match, the Griffins launched a final assault, pushing deeper into Owl territory. The Owls' defense held strong, but the Griffins were determined to break through.

Ellie, now battle-tested and confident in her abilities, rallied her teammates. "This is our moment, Owls. We've faced tough opponents before, and we've overcome every challenge together. Let's show them what the Owls are made of!"

Her teammates nodded in agreement, their determination matching Ellie's. They knew that this was a defining moment, a test of their resilience and teamwork.

As the Griffins continued to advance, the Owls' defense tightened. The Griffins tried one final push, but the Owls held firm. With a collective effort, they forced a turnover in possession.

The referee's whistle blew, signaling the change in possession. The Owls had the ball, and they knew that this was their chance to secure victory. With a series of quick passes and strategic moves, they worked their way toward the Griffins' try line.

Ellie, once again, led the final charge. She sprinted toward the try line with the ball in hand, the Griffins' defense closing in. But Ellie had learned that the real magic of rugby was in the belief in one's own abilities and the strength of teamwork.

With a burst of energy, she dived for the try line, stretching out her arm with all her might. The stadium erupted in cheers as the referee's whistle blew, confirming the try. The Owls had secured a hard-fought victory.

Ellie's teammates rushed to her, lifting her onto their shoulders in celebration. Coach Wilson beamed with pride as she watched her team's triumphant moment.

"You did it, Owls," Coach Wilson said. "You faced a tough opponent, and you proved that with hard work, dedication, and teamwork, you can overcome any challenge. This victory belongs to all of you."

As the Owls celebrated their victory, Ellie couldn't help but reflect on her journey. She had come a long way from the shy girl who had stumbled upon a pair of magical rugby boots. She had discovered the true magic of rugby – the power of teamwork, determination, and the belief in oneself.

The story of Ellie and her teammates became a source of inspiration for their small town of Oakridge. It was a reminder that true greatness could be achieved through hard work and unity. The Owls continued to play the game they loved, not as individuals with magical boots, but as a team that played with heart and soul.

And as Ellie looked at her teammates, their smiles reflecting the joy of their hard-earned victory, she knew that she had found her place in the world of rugby. The magic of the game was not in the boots; it was in the friendships, the challenges, and the victories that they shared as a team.

The championship victory was just the beginning of Ellie's rugby journey. She continued to play the game she loved, not as the girl with the magical boots but as a dedicated and passionate rugby player. Her skills continued to improve, and she became a role model for young rugby enthusiasts in Oakridge.

As the years passed, Ellie's love for rugby remained unwavering. She played for her school, her town, and eventually, she earned a spot on the regional girls' rugby team. Her journey had come full circle, from a shy girl with a pair of magical boots to a confident and skilled rugby player.

One sunny afternoon, after a particularly satisfying victory with her regional team, Ellie decided it was time to have a conversation with Mr. Higgins, the kindly sports shop owner who had sold her the magical boots. She wanted to thank him for introducing her to rugby and for the incredible journey she had embarked on.

As Ellie entered the small sports shop, she saw Mr. Higgins behind the counter, organizing a stack of rugby balls. He looked up and smiled warmly when he saw Ellie.

"Ellie! What brings you here today?" he asked.

"I wanted to talk to you about the magic rugby boots," Ellie replied.

Mr. Higgins nodded and motioned for her to sit on a nearby bench. "Ah, those boots have quite a story, don't they? How have they been treating you?"

Ellie smiled, thinking back on her journey. "They've been amazing, Mr. Higgins. They helped me discover my love for rugby, and I've had some incredible experiences. But I've also learned that the real magic of rugby is in hard work, dedication, and teamwork."

Mr. Higgins nodded thoughtfully. "You've learned a valuable lesson, Ellie. The boots can give you a boost, but it's your passion and commitment that truly make the difference."

"I couldn't agree more," Ellie said. "I wanted to thank you for introducing me to rugby and for selling me those boots. They were the starting point of an amazing journey."

Mr. Higgins smiled and reached under the counter, pulling out a neatly wrapped package. "I have something for you, Ellie."

Curious, Ellie accepted the package and unwrapped it. Inside was a brand-new pair of rugby boots, not magical like the old ones but sturdy and well-made.

"These are for you, Ellie," Mr. Higgins said. "A gift to support your continued journey in rugby. Remember, the magic is in you, not the boots."

Touched by the gesture, Ellie thanked Mr. Higgins and promised to continue working hard and giving her best on the rugby field.

As Ellie left the sports shop with her new boots in hand, she couldn't help but feel grateful for the incredible journey she had experienced. The magic rugby boots had been the catalyst, but her dedication, teamwork, and belief in herself had carried her through.

Years passed, and Ellie's love for rugby only grew stronger. She played at the national level, representing her country in international tournaments. She became a rugby legend, known not for magical boots but for her unwavering passion and talent.

But Ellie never forgot the lesson she had learned as a young girl in Oakridge – that true magic was not in external gifts but in the belief in oneself and the power of teamwork. And whenever she stepped onto the rugby field, she carried that lesson with her, inspiring others to believe in themselves and reach for the stars.

The End.

Try for the Stars

Part 1

In the heart of a small Welsh town named Brynmawr, nestled among rolling hills and surrounded by lush green fields, lived an 11-year-old girl named Megan. She was a spirited and determined young girl with a deep passion for rugby. The sound of a rugby ball hitting the ground and the cheers of the crowd as they watched the local boys' team play filled her with a sense of exhilaration.

Megan's family had a long history of rugby enthusiasts, and her father often took her to watch matches at the town's rugby club. As she watched the players sprint down the field, tackle their opponents, and score tries, a dream took root in Megan's heart. She wanted to play rugby too, to feel the adrenaline rush of the game, to experience the camaraderie of being on a team, and to make her family proud.

However, Megan quickly discovered that there was a significant obstacle in her path. Her school, Brynmawr Primary, didn't have a girls' rugby team. It seemed that rugby was reserved solely for the boys, and Megan felt a deep sense of disappointment.

One chilly autumn morning, as Megan sat on the swings in the school playground, her best friend, Rhys, approached her with a curious look on his face. Rhys had been her friend since they were toddlers, and they shared many of the same interests, including a love for rugby.

"Hey, Megan," Rhys said, "I heard they're starting a rugby club for the boys in our year. It's going to be awesome!"

Megan frowned, feeling a pang of envy. "That sounds great, Rhys. I wish I could join, but they're only letting the boys play."

Rhys tilted his head thoughtfully. "Why don't you talk to Mrs. Evans, our PE teacher? Maybe she can help."

Megan's eyes brightened at the suggestion. Mrs. Evans was known for her fairness and her support for all students, regardless of their gender. Megan decided to give it a try.

The next day, after school, Megan gathered her courage and approached Mrs. Evans in the gymnasium. The PE teacher was busy organizing equipment, but she greeted Megan with a warm smile.

"Hello, Megan," Mrs. Evans said. "What can I do for you?"

Megan took a deep breath and spoke earnestly. "Mrs. Evans, I really love rugby, and I want to play. But they're only letting the boys join the rugby club. Can't girls play rugby too?"

Mrs. Evans paused for a moment, considering Megan's request. She saw the determination in the young girl's eyes and realized that this could be an opportunity to promote equality and inclusion.

"You know, Megan," Mrs. Evans said thoughtfully, "there's no reason why girls can't play rugby. It's just that we haven't had a girls' team here before. But if you're willing to gather some girls who are interested, I'd be more than happy to coach you."

Megan's heart soared with excitement. She knew that this was the first step toward realizing her dream. She thanked Mrs. Evans profusely and hurriedly left the gym, determined to assemble a team of girls who shared her passion for rugby.

Over the next few days, Megan went to work recruiting her teammates. She approached girls from different backgrounds and with diverse interests, all of whom had never played rugby before. Megan believed that with determination, hard work, and a little bit of coaching, they could form a formidable team.

Her first recruit was Amelia, a bookworm with a knack for strategy. Amelia loved reading about legendary sports figures and saw this as an opportunity to be a part of her own sports story. Then came Lily, an artist with a creative mind. She was drawn to rugby's physicality and saw it as a way to express herself in a new and exciting way.

Megan also convinced Sarah, a budding musician with a passion for rhythm and coordination, to join. Sarah saw the rugby field as a canvas where she could create her own masterpieces of movement and teamwork. Lastly, there was Amina, a girl from a different cultural background who had never played rugby but was eager to embrace this new experience.

Together, Megan, Amelia, Lily, Sarah, and Amina approached Mrs. Evans with their proposal. They explained their dreams of forming a girls' rugby team, showcasing their determination and passion for the sport.

Mrs. Evans, impressed by their enthusiasm, agreed to become their coach. She realized that this endeavor could be an opportunity to break stereotypes and pave the way for future generations of girls who aspired to play rugby.

With Mrs. Evans on board, Megan and her friends set out to overcome the challenges that lay ahead. They faced the hurdle of a lack of equipment and rugby gear, but they were undeterred. They scoured garage sales, asked for donations from their families, and even held a bake sale to raise funds to purchase the necessary gear.

Their efforts paid off, and soon they had a collection of rugby balls, jerseys, and boots. They were ready to embark on their rugby journey, but little did they know that their biggest challenges were still ahead.

As Megan and her newly formed team began their training, they faced skepticism from some of the boys' rugby teams at school.

The boys didn't take the girls seriously and often made snide remarks about their abilities.

During one particularly challenging practice session, Megan and her teammates were practicing their passing and tackling when a group of boys from the boys' rugby club approached. They watched with condescending smirks on their faces.

"Look at them trying to play rugby," one of the boys scoffed. "Girls will never be as good as us."

Megan felt her cheeks flush with anger, but she refused to let the taunts deter her. She had a dream, and she was determined to prove that girls could excel in rugby just as much as boys.

Mrs. Evans stepped in, addressing the boys firmly. "Rugby is a sport for everyone, regardless of gender. Megan and her teammates have just as much right to be on this field as you do. Let's respect each other and focus on our training."

The boys grumbled but eventually left, realizing that their comments weren't going to discourage Megan and her team.

The girls continued their training, facing numerous challenges along the way. They struggled to master the basics of passing, tackling, and teamwork. There were times when they felt discouraged, but Megan's unwavering determination and Mrs. Evans' coaching skills kept them going.

Part 2

Megan and her newly formed girls' rugby team, which they had proudly named the "Brynmawr Stars," embarked on a journey filled with determination, challenges, and the unwavering belief that they could overcome any obstacle in their path.

Their training began in earnest, with Mrs. Evans guiding them through the basics of rugby. The girls practiced passing the ball to each other, perfecting their throws, and working on their ball-handling skills. They also learned the art of tackling and defending, though it was initially met with hesitation and nervousness.

One sunny afternoon, as the girls gathered on the school's rugby field, Megan addressed her teammates with an encouraging smile. "Okay, Stars, today we're going to work on tackling. Remember, we're a team, and we're here to support each other. Let's give it our all!"

They paired off and began practicing tackling techniques. Amina, who had never played rugby before, was initially hesitant. However, Megan, always the supportive leader, demonstrated the tackle with patience and encouragement, helping Amina build confidence in her abilities.

Amelia, the strategic thinker of the group, had been reading rugby books and studying the sport's techniques. She shared her insights on tackling, adding a layer of intelligence to their physical training. Lily's artistic eye helped the team understand body positioning and leverage, allowing them to execute tackles with precision.

Despite their initial apprehensions, the girls soon realized that tackling was not about brute force alone; it was about technique, timing, and working together as a team. They supported each other, offering feedback and encouragement with each successful tackle.

As weeks passed, the Brynmawr Stars faced the challenge of limited training time. The boys' rugby club had priority on the field, leaving the girls with only a few hours each week to practice. Still, they made the most of their time, arriving early and staying late, determined to catch up with the boys' teams.

One crisp morning, as they practiced their lineouts, the girls encountered another obstacle. They didn't have proper rugby posts to practice with. Undeterred, Megan came up with an ingenious idea. She and her father, who had always been a rugby enthusiast, constructed makeshift rugby posts using PVC pipes and sandbags. It wasn't ideal, but it allowed them to continue training.

Their resourcefulness and dedication began to attract attention. Some of the boys' rugby players, who had initially mocked them, started showing a begrudging respect for the Brynmawr Stars.

They could see that these girls were not backing down, and their determination was slowly earning them the respect they deserved.

One day, during a practice match with one of the boys' teams, Megan's team faced teasing and taunts from their opponents. They were determined to prove themselves, and although they lost the match, they scored a try and held their own on the field. The boys were surprised by the girls' resilience and began to treat them with a newfound respect.

However, not everyone was supportive. Megan and her friends faced skepticism from some of the girls in their school. "Girls don't play rugby," they would say, echoing stereotypes they had grown up with. It hurt, but Megan and her team refused to let these comments deter them. They knew that they were breaking barriers and paving the way for other girls who dreamt of playing rugby.

Megan also faced doubts within herself at times. She felt the weight of responsibility as the team's captain and leader. There were moments when she questioned whether she was doing enough to lead her team to success. However, her father always reminded her of the importance of perseverance and believing in herself.

"You're a star, Megan," he would say with a proud smile. "And stars never stop shining, no matter how tough the journey gets."

Megan's father's words resonated with her, and she resolved to lead her team with even greater determination. She knew that their journey was just beginning, and there would be more challenges ahead.

One sunny afternoon, after a grueling practice, the Brynmawr Stars gathered in the school's cafeteria for a well-deserved snack. They shared laughter, sandwiches, and stories of their progress. Megan couldn't help but feel a swell of pride for her team and the bond they had formed.

"We've come a long way, haven't we?" Amelia remarked, her eyes shining with pride.

Lily nodded in agreement. "Yes, and we're not stopping here. We're going to show everyone what we're capable of."

As they continued to train and improve, the Brynmawr Stars began to form a close-knit sisterhood. They supported each other not only on the rugby field but also in their personal lives. They shared their dreams, fears, and aspirations, forging a friendship that transcended rugby.

Sarah, who had initially been hesitant about tackling and had struggled to find her place on the team, discovered her talent for quick thinking and adaptability. She became the team's scrum-half, orchestrating plays with precision. Her teammates admired her ability to assess the situation on the field and make split-second decisions.

Amina's agility and speed made her a natural winger, while Lily's creativity allowed her to come up with innovative ways to approach the game. Amelia's strategic thinking made her an invaluable asset, and Megan's leadership and determination shone through every practice and match.

Mrs. Evans was amazed by the progress the girls had made. She had been a rugby coach for many years, but coaching the Brynmawr Stars held a special place in her heart. She admired their resilience, determination, and the way they challenged stereotypes about girls in sports.

One evening, after a particularly challenging practice, Mrs. Evans gathered the girls around. "I want to share something with you," she began, her eyes filled with pride. "Throughout history, there have been incredible women who broke barriers in the world of sports. Women like Billie Jean King, who fought for gender equality in tennis, or Mia Hamm, one of the greatest soccer players of all time."

The girls listened intently, inspired by the stories of these pioneering women. Mrs. Evans continued, "You, my dear Brynmawr Stars, are also pioneers. You're breaking barriers right here in our town. And someday, young girls will look up to you and say, 'Because of them, I can play rugby too.'"

The words resonated with the girls, filling them with a sense of purpose and pride. They were not just playing rugby; they were setting an example for others and proving that with determination, hard work, and support, they could achieve anything.

As the weeks turned into months, the Brynmawr Stars' skills improved significantly. They began to challenge other schools' girls' teams to friendly matches, slowly gaining recognition and respect in the local rugby community. They faced victories and losses, but their determination never wavered.

One sunny afternoon, as they practiced their scrums, Mrs. Evans announced some exciting news. "I've entered us into a girls' rugby tournament," she said, her eyes sparkling with enthusiasm. "It's a chance for us to test our skills against other teams from the region."

The girls cheered with excitement, realizing that their first official match was on the horizon. They couldn't wait to show everyone how far they had come since their humble beginnings.

The day of their first official match arrived, and the Brynmawr Stars felt a mixture of nerves and excitement. They were about to step onto the field as a team, ready to face other girls' rugby teams from the region.

The match was tough, and the Brynmawr Stars had their fair share of challenges. They made mistakes, missed tackles, and faced moments of doubt. But they never stopped fighting, and their determination shone through.

In the final moments of the match, with the score tied, Megan saw an opportunity. She executed a perfect pass to Amina, who sprinted down the field, leaving the opposing team in her wake. With a burst of speed, Amina scored the winning try, and the Brynmawr Stars emerged victorious.

The girls celebrated their first official win with tears of joy and laughter. They realized that they had not only won the match but also the respect of their peers and the local rugby community. It was a defining moment in their journey.

As word of their victory spread, the Brynmawr Stars received praise and support from their school and the community. The boys' rugby teams, who had once teased them, now acknowledged their skills and dedication. The girls in their school who had doubted them began to see them as role models.

Part 3

The taste of victory lingered in the air as the Brynmawr Stars celebrated their first official win. The joy and pride they felt were indescribable. They had faced skepticism, challenges, and doubt, but their determination had brought them triumph. However, as they soon learned, success in sports was not always a smooth ascent to the top.

Following their first victory, the Brynmawr Stars continued to train diligently, refining their skills and teamwork. Mrs. Evans, their dedicated coach, knew that this was just the beginning of their journey. She emphasized the importance of consistency and hard work, reminding them that every win came from countless hours of practice.

The girls faced various schools in friendly matches, some of which they won, and others they lost. Every match was a learning experience, teaching them valuable lessons about strategy, endurance, and the importance of staying calm under pressure.

As their reputation grew, so did their confidence. The support from their families, schoolmates, and even some of the boys' rugby teams motivated them to push their boundaries further. Megan, with her unwavering determination, emerged as a natural leader. She encouraged her teammates, inspired them to persevere, and led by example.

However, they knew that their biggest challenge lay ahead—the first official tournament. It was a regional event, where they would compete against highly skilled girls' rugby teams from neighboring towns and schools. Winning this tournament would not only be a testament to their abilities but also a significant milestone in their journey to break barriers and earn respect in the world of rugby.

The days leading up to the tournament were filled with intense training sessions, team bonding, and mental preparation. Mrs. Evans had them practice scenarios and strategies that they might encounter during the matches. They drilled tirelessly, honing their skills and developing a unique style of play that leveraged their diverse strengths.

Amina's speed and agility made her a formidable winger, capable of weaving through the opposition with ease. Lily's creative thinking allowed her to come up with innovative plays that caught their opponents off guard. Amelia's strategic approach made her an invaluable decision-maker on the field, while Sarah's quick thinking and coordination were vital in orchestrating their plays.

Their teamwork was impeccable. They communicated seamlessly on the field, anticipating each other's moves and supporting one another in times of need. It was this synergy that set the Brynmawr Stars apart from the competition.

On the morning of the tournament, the girls gathered at the school's rugby field, their hearts filled with a mixture of excitement and nerves. They donned their green and white jerseys with pride, a symbol of their unity and determination.

Megan addressed her teammates with a pep talk that reflected her unwavering belief in their abilities. "Remember, we've come a long way, and we're not just a team; we're the Brynmawr Stars! Let's show everyone what we're made of and play our hearts out!"

With their coach, Mrs. Evans, by their side, the girls boarded the bus that would take them to the tournament venue. They felt a sense of camaraderie and determination, ready to face whatever challenges awaited them.

As they arrived at the tournament grounds, the Brynmawr Stars couldn't help but feel a sense of awe. The field was alive with activity, with teams from different schools warming up, practicing their drills, and strategizing. It was a sea of green and white jerseys, a testament to the passion and dedication of girls' rugby teams from the region.

Their first match was against a team from a neighboring town. The tension was palpable as they stepped onto the field, the cheers of the crowd ringing in their ears. Megan looked at her teammates, their faces a mix of excitement and determination. They were ready to prove themselves.

The whistle blew, and the match began. It was a fiercely contested battle, with both teams displaying impressive skills and determination. The Brynmawr Stars executed their plays with precision, showcasing their teamwork and commitment.

Amina's speed allowed her to make remarkable runs down the wing, while Lily's creativity led to innovative plays that kept their opponents guessing. Sarah's quick thinking and coordination ensured that their passes were accurate, and Amelia's strategic decision-making helped them maintain control of the game.

Despite their best efforts, the match ended in a draw. While they hadn't won, the Brynmawr Stars knew that they had given their all. They were proud of their performance and knew that they had earned the respect of their opponents.

The tournament continued, with the Brynmawr Stars facing different teams throughout the day. Some matches they won, others they lost, but their determination remained unwavering. Each game was a chance to learn, adapt, and grow as a team.

As they progressed through the rounds, the Brynmawr Stars faced teams with varying styles of play. Some were fast and agile, while others were strong and physical. Each match presented unique challenges, forcing the girls to adjust their strategies and tactics on the fly.

Their resilience and teamwork shone through as they battled through the rounds, surprising everyone with their determination and skill. They were no longer just the underdogs; they were a force to be reckoned with.

The final match of the tournament was a tense showdown against a seasoned team that had a reputation for their strong defense and strategic play. The Brynmawr Stars were the underdogs, and the pressure was palpable. However, they refused to let the weight of expectations crush their spirits.

The match began, and both teams fought fiercely for dominance. The Brynmawr Stars displayed exceptional teamwork and determination, holding their own against the seasoned opponents. The crowd watched in awe as the girls executed plays with precision and tackled their opponents with unwavering commitment.

As the match entered its final minutes, the score remained tied. Megan knew that this was their moment to shine, their chance to prove that they could overcome the odds. With a burst of energy and determination, she made a decisive play, setting up a perfect pass to Amina, who sprinted toward the try line with lightning speed.

Amina's try, in the closing moments of the match, secured victory for the Brynmawr Stars. The final whistle blew, and the girls celebrated their hard-earned triumph. They had won the tournament, a remarkable achievement that had seemed impossible just a short while ago.

The crowd erupted in cheers and applause, recognizing the determination and skill displayed by the Brynmawr Stars. The girls were overwhelmed with emotion, hugging each other tightly and relishing their victory.

As they stood on the podium to receive their trophy, Megan couldn't help but reflect on their incredible journey. They had faced doubt, challenges, and adversity, but they had emerged victorious, earning the respect and admiration of their peers and the rugby community.

Their journey had been about more than just winning matches; it had been about breaking barriers, proving that girls could excel in rugby, and forging friendships that would last a lifetime. The Brynmawr Stars had become pioneers, inspiring other girls to follow their dreams and showing that with determination, hard work, and unwavering belief, they could reach for the stars.

The celebration continued long into the night, with the Brynmawr Stars basking in the glory of their victory. They knew that their journey was far from over, but they were ready to face whatever challenges lay ahead. They had proven that they were stars, and stars never stopped shining, no matter how tough the journey got.

Part 4

The triumph at the regional tournament had left the Brynmawr Stars elated, their spirits soaring higher than ever before. Their remarkable journey had not only earned them recognition but had also ignited a fire within each of them. They were no longer just a girls' rugby team from a small Welsh town; they were a symbol of determination, teamwork, and the relentless pursuit of dreams.

Their victory had brought them closer as a team, and their bond had grown even stronger. They practiced with renewed vigor, refining their skills and building on the strategies that had propelled them to success. Each member of the team had found their niche, their unique role on the field that contributed to the Brynmawr Stars' exceptional play.

Amina, the speedy winger, had become known for her dazzling runs down the field, leaving opposing defenders in her dust. She had mastered the art of sidestepping and had a knack for finding gaps in the defense. Her ability to change direction with lightning speed had earned her the nickname "The Gazelle" among her teammates.

Lily's creative thinking continued to be a valuable asset to the team. She had a knack for coming up with innovative plays that caught their opponents off guard. Her vision on the field was unparalleled, and her passes were a work of art. Lily had become the team's playmaker, setting up scoring opportunities with her brilliant strategy.

Amelia's strategic prowess had only grown, and she had become the team's decision-maker during matches. Her ability to read the game, anticipate opponents' moves, and make quick decisions had saved the team on numerous occasions. Megan often turned to Amelia for guidance during high-pressure moments, knowing that her friend's strategic mind would lead them to victory.

Sarah, who had initially struggled with tackling, had blossomed into an all-around player. Her quick thinking and coordination had made her an essential part of the team's defense and attack. She had found her place as a versatile player, capable of adapting to various positions as needed. Sarah's journey from uncertainty to confidence had inspired the entire team.

Megan, as the team's captain and leader, continued to shine both on and off the field. Her unwavering determination and commitment set the standard for the Brynmawr Stars. She led by example, always pushing herself to be the best, and motivating her teammates to do the same. Megan had grown into a respected leader, admired by her teammates for her dedication and strength.

Their training sessions were now more focused and structured, with Mrs. Evans fine-tuning their skills and strategies. The girls practiced tirelessly, honing their abilities and perfecting their plays. Their dedication to improvement was unwavering, and they knew that their journey was far from over.

With their growing confidence, the Brynmawr Stars continued to challenge themselves by playing against stronger opponents. They faced teams from larger towns and schools, teams that had a rich rugby tradition and a history of success. It was a daunting task, but the girls were undaunted.

Their first match against a formidable opponent was a test of their abilities. The opposing team had a reputation for their physicality and aggressive playstyle. As the match began, the Brynmawr Stars found themselves in a fierce battle.

The opposing team's size and strength were evident, but the Brynmawr Stars refused to back down. They relied on their teamwork, agility, and strategic play to counter their opponents' advantages. It was a grueling match, with both teams pushing their limits.

In the final moments of the game, with the score tied, it was Megan who seized the opportunity. With a burst of speed and determination, she broke through the opposing defense and scored the winning try. The Brynmawr Stars emerged victorious once again, proving that their success was not a fluke.

The girls celebrated their hard-fought win, their cheers echoing across the field. The opposing team, despite their defeat, acknowledged the Brynmawr Stars' exceptional skills and sportsmanship. It was a testament to the progress the girls had made and the respect they had earned in the rugby community.

Word of their victory spread, and the Brynmawr Stars began receiving invitations to participate in various tournaments and events. They were no longer just a local sensation; they were gaining recognition on a regional level. Megan and her teammates relished the opportunity to compete against the best teams in the area, knowing that every match was a chance to grow and improve.

As their reputation continued to grow, the Brynmawr Stars received support from unexpected sources. The boys' rugby teams at their school, who had once doubted and teased them, now viewed them as equals. They offered to share the rugby field for practice sessions, fostering a sense of unity and camaraderie among the students.

The girls in their school who had initially doubted them had also changed their perspective. Many of them had attended the Brynmawr Stars' matches and had witnessed the team's determination and skill firsthand. They now looked up to Megan and her teammates as role models, and some of them even expressed an interest in joining the rugby team in the future.

The Brynmawr Stars' success had a ripple effect throughout the community. Parents, teachers, and local rugby enthusiasts rallied behind the girls, attending their matches and providing support. The local newspaper featured the team in a heartwarming article, highlighting their journey from humble beginnings to regional recognition.

Their success also caught the attention of a local business owner who offered to sponsor the Brynmawr Stars. With the financial support, the team was able to invest in better equipment, hire specialized coaches for additional training, and travel to tournaments further afield. The sponsorship was a testament to the impact the girls had made in their town.

Despite their growing success, Megan and her teammates remained grounded. They knew that their journey was a marathon, not a sprint, and that they still had much to learn and achieve. They continued to attend practices with enthusiasm, eager to improve and face new challenges.

One day, as they gathered for practice, Mrs. Evans shared some exciting news. "The South Wales Girls' Rugby Championship is coming up," she announced. "It's a prestigious tournament, and we've been invited to participate. This is a chance to compete against some of the best girls' rugby teams in the region."

The girls' faces lit up with excitement at the prospect of such a prestigious event. The South Wales Girls' Rugby Championship was a significant tournament, and an invitation to participate was a testament to their growing reputation.

Megan, always the steadfast leader, addressed her teammates with a determined expression. "This is our chance to shine on an even bigger stage, to prove that the Brynmawr Stars are a force to be reckoned with. Let's give it our all and show everyone what we're made of!"

The girls embarked on rigorous training sessions in preparation for the championship. They worked on their physical conditioning, honed their skills, and refined their strategies. Mrs. Evans introduced new drills and exercises to challenge them further, ensuring they were well-prepared for the competition.

In the weeks leading up to the championship, the Brynmawr Stars faced strong opponents in practice matches. They welcomed the opportunity to test themselves against teams with different playing styles and strategies. Each practice match was a chance to learn, adapt, and refine their tactics.

The day of the South Wales Girls' Rugby Championship arrived, and the Brynmawr Stars were filled with a mix of anticipation and nerves. They knew that the competition would be fierce, and they were prepared to face the best teams in the region.

As they stepped onto the tournament grounds, they were greeted by the sight of teams from all over South Wales, each wearing their distinctive jerseys. The atmosphere was charged with excitement and anticipation. Megan and her teammates wore their green and white jerseys with pride, representing Brynmawr with honor.

Their first match in the championship was against a team that had a reputation for their powerful forwards and dominant scrums. The Brynmawr Stars were up against a formidable opponent, and the match would test their skills and resilience to the fullest.

The game was intense from the start, with both teams displaying incredible determination and commitment. The Brynmawr Stars relied on their agility and strategic play to counter the opposing team's physicality. It was a hard-fought battle, with neither team giving an inch.

In the closing minutes of the match, with the score tied, it was Amina who once again showcased her incredible speed. She broke through the defense with a burst of acceleration, leaving her opponents behind. With a graceful dive, she scored the winning try, securing victory for the Brynmawr Stars.

The girls celebrated their hard-earned win, their cheers echoing through the tournament grounds. The opposing team, despite their defeat, acknowledged the Brynmawr Stars' exceptional skills and sportsmanship. It was a defining moment in the championship, and the Brynmawr Stars had proven that they belonged among the best.

As the tournament progressed, the Brynmawr Stars faced a series of challenging matches. They battled teams with different strengths and strategies, adapting and learning with each game. Their teamwork and determination remained unwavering, and they continued to showcase their exceptional skills on the field.

In the final match of the championship, the Brynmawr Stars found themselves facing a seasoned team with a history of success. The pressure was immense, but Megan and her teammates were undaunted. They had come so far on their journey, and they were determined to give it their all.

The match was a fierce contest, with both teams displaying remarkable skill and determination. The Brynmawr Stars relied on their strategic play and teamwork to hold their own against their formidable opponents. It was a thrilling and intense battle that kept the crowd on the edge of their seats.

As the final moments of the match approached, with the score tied, it was Megan who once again seized the opportunity. With a burst of speed and determination, she executed a perfect pass to Amina, who sprinted toward the try line with lightning speed. Amina's try secured victory for the Brynmawr Stars, and the final whistle blew.

The girls celebrated their hard-fought win, their cheers filling the air. They had won the South Wales Girls' Rugby Championship, a remarkable achievement that had seemed improbable at the start of their journey. Their triumph was a testament to their unwavering dedication, resilience, and belief in themselves.

The crowd erupted in applause, recognizing the exceptional skill and sportsmanship displayed by the Brynmawr Stars. The girls stood on the podium to receive their championship trophy, their hearts filled with pride and gratitude. They had not only achieved victory but had also earned the respect and admiration of the rugby community.

The celebration continued long into the night, with the Brynmawr Stars basking in the glory of their championship win. They knew that their journey was far from over, and they would face new challenges in the future. However, they were united as a team, as pioneers of girls' rugby in Brynmawr, and as symbols of what could be achieved with determination, hard work, and unwavering belief.

Megan, standing with her teammates, reflected on their incredible journey. She knew that their success was not just about winning matches; it was about breaking barriers and forging a path for other girls who dreamt of playing rugby. It was about proving that with determination and teamwork, they could reach for the stars and achieve their goals.

The Brynmawr Stars had become a beacon of inspiration in their town, a symbol of what could be accomplished when individuals came together as a team and pursued their dreams with unwavering passion. They had shown that they were not just stars; they were champions, and their light would continue to shine brightly, guiding others to reach for their own dreams.

Part 5

The Brynmawr Stars had achieved incredible success, winning the South Wales Girls' Rugby Championship. Their journey had been nothing short of remarkable, and their determination, teamwork, and unwavering belief in themselves had brought them to this moment. However, their story was far from over, and they faced their next challenge with determination and unity.

As champions, the Brynmawr Stars received an invitation to participate in the South Wales Regional Girls' Rugby Tournament. It was a prestigious event, featuring highly skilled teams from all over South Wales. The girls were excited, but they knew that the competition would be fierce.

In the weeks leading up to the tournament, the Brynmawr Stars intensified their training sessions. They worked on their conditioning, refined their skills, and fine-tuned their strategies. Mrs. Evans, their dedicated coach, pushed them to their limits, ensuring they were well-prepared for the upcoming challenges.

The tournament day arrived, and the girls were filled with a mix of excitement and nerves. They knew that they were facing some of the best girls' rugby teams in the region, and the pressure was palpable. However, they had faced adversity before and had emerged victorious.

As they stepped onto the tournament grounds, they were greeted by the sight of teams from various towns and schools, each sporting their distinctive jerseys. The atmosphere was charged with anticipation, and the girls wore their green and white jerseys with pride, representing Brynmawr with honor.

Their first match in the tournament was against a team known for their speed and agility. The game was intense from the start, with both teams displaying remarkable determination and skill. The Brynmawr Stars relied on their strategic play and teamwork to counter their opponents' swiftness.

Amina, with her lightning speed, dazzled on the wing, making remarkable runs down the field. Lily's creative thinking led to innovative plays that kept their opponents guessing. Amelia's strategic decision-making helped them maintain control of the game, and Sarah's quick thinking and coordination ensured their passes were accurate.

Megan, as the team's captain, led by example, pushing herself to be the best and motivating her teammates to do the same. She was a force to be reckoned with on the field, showcasing her determination and leadership.

The match was closely contested, with both teams refusing to give an inch. In the final moments, it was Lily who seized the opportunity. With a brilliant move, she broke through the opposing defense and scored the winning try. The Brynmawr

Stars emerged victorious, their first match in the tournament ending in triumph.

The girls celebrated their hard-fought win, their cheers echoing through the tournament grounds. The opposing team, despite their defeat, acknowledged the Brynmawr Stars' exceptional skills and sportsmanship. It was a promising start to the tournament, and the girls knew that they were up for the challenge.

As the tournament continued, the Brynmawr Stars faced a series of challenging matches. They battled teams with different strengths and strategies, adapting and learning with each game. Their teamwork and determination remained unwavering, and they continued to showcase their exceptional skills on the field.

Their resilience was put to the test in a match against a team known for their physicality and strong forwards. It was a grueling battle, with both teams engaging in fierce scrums and hard tackles. The Brynmawr Stars, despite being the smaller team, refused to be intimidated.

Amelia's strategic decision-making and Megan's leadership were instrumental in keeping the team organized and focused. Amina's speed allowed her to make remarkable runs down the wing, while Lily's creative thinking led to innovative plays that countered their opponents' strength.

In the closing moments of the match, with the score tied, it was Sarah who made a crucial tackle, preventing the opposing team from scoring. The girls rallied, launching a counterattack that led to Megan scoring the winning try. The Brynmawr Stars emerged victorious once again, their determination and teamwork prevailing.

The crowd watched in awe as the Brynmawr Stars celebrated their hard-fought win. The opposing team, despite their defeat, acknowledged the girls' exceptional skills and sportsmanship. It was a testament to the progress the Brynmawr Stars had made and the respect they had earned in the rugby community.

Their journey through the tournament was not without its challenges. They faced teams with varying styles of play, some relying on speed and agility, while others favored a more physical approach. Each match presented unique obstacles, forcing the girls to adapt and adjust their strategies.

One of the defining moments of the tournament came in a match against a team known for their strong defense and strategic play. The Brynmawr Stars were the underdogs, facing a team that had a reputation for their disciplined approach to the game.

The match was a tense battle, with both teams displaying incredible determination and skill. The Brynmawr Stars relied on their strategic play and teamwork to break through the opposing defense. Amelia's decision-making and Megan's leadership were vital in keeping the team focused and organized.

As the match entered its final minutes, with the score tied, it was Amina who once again showcased her incredible speed. She executed a perfect pass from Megan, sprinting toward the try line with lightning speed. Amina's try secured victory for the Brynmawr Stars, and the final whistle blew.

The girls celebrated their hard-earned win, their cheers filling the air. The opposing team, despite their defeat, acknowledged the Brynmawr Stars' exceptional skills and sportsmanship. It was a defining moment in the tournament, and the Brynmawr Stars had proven that they could compete at the highest level.

As they progressed through the rounds, the Brynmawr Stars found themselves in the tournament final. They were about to face a seasoned team with a history of success in girls' rugby. The pressure was immense, but the girls were undaunted. They knew that they had come so far on their journey, and they were determined to give it their all.

The final match of the tournament was a nail-biting showdown, with both teams displaying remarkable skill and determination. The Brynmawr Stars relied on their strategic play and teamwork to hold their own against their seasoned opponents. It was a thrilling and intense battle that kept the crowd on the edge of their seats.

In the final moments of the match, with the score tied, it was Lily who seized the opportunity. With a brilliant move, she broke through the opposing defense and scored the winning try. The Brynmawr Stars emerged victorious, their determination and teamwork prevailing once again.

The girls celebrated their hard-fought win, their cheers echoing through the tournament grounds. They had won the South Wales Regional Girls' Rugby Tournament, a remarkable achievement that had seemed improbable at the start of their journey. Their triumph was a testament to their unwavering dedication, resilience, and belief in themselves.

The crowd erupted in applause, recognizing the exceptional skill and sportsmanship displayed by the Brynmawr Stars. The girls stood on the podium to receive their championship trophy, their hearts filled with pride and gratitude. They had not only achieved victory but had also earned the respect and admiration of the rugby community.

The celebration continued long into the night, with the Brynmawr Stars basking in the glory of their championship win. They knew that their journey was far from over, and they would face new challenges in the future. However, they were united as a team, as pioneers of girls' rugby in Brynmawr, and as symbols of what could be achieved with determination, hard work, and unwavering belief.

Megan, standing with her teammates, reflected on their incredible journey. She knew that their success was not just about winning matches; it was about breaking barriers and forging a path for other girls who dreamt of playing rugby. It was about proving that with determination and teamwork, they could reach for the stars and achieve their goals.

The Brynmawr Stars had become a beacon of inspiration in their town, a symbol of what could be accomplished when individuals came together as a team and pursued their dreams with unwavering passion. They had shown that they were not just stars; they were champions, and their light would continue to shine brightly, guiding others to reach for their own dreams.

Part 6

The Brynmawr Stars had achieved an incredible victory in the South Wales Regional Girls' Rugby Tournament. Their journey from a group of determined girls with a dream to champions of the region had been nothing short of remarkable. However, their triumph was not only about winning matches but also about breaking barriers, earning respect, and inspiring others to follow their dreams.

As the final whistle blew in the championship match, the Brynmawr Stars celebrated their hard-earned win. The crowd erupted in cheers and applause, recognizing the exceptional skill and sportsmanship displayed by the team. They had not only emerged victorious but had also earned the respect and admiration of the rugby community.

The girls stood on the podium to receive their championship trophy, their faces beaming with pride and gratitude. It was a moment they had dreamed of, a moment that marked the culmination of their relentless dedication and unwavering belief in themselves.

The championship trophy was a symbol of their triumph, but it was also a symbol of the barriers they had broken. They had shown that girls could excel in rugby, that they could compete at the highest level, and that they could earn the respect of their peers and the rugby community.

The celebration continued long into the night, with the Brynmawr Stars basking in the glory of their championship win. Their families, friends, and supporters joined them in their joyous revelry. It was a night filled with laughter, cheers, and heartfelt speeches.

Mrs. Evans, their dedicated coach, addressed the team with pride and admiration. "You've achieved something truly remarkable," she said. "You've shown that with determination, hard work, and belief in yourselves, you can accomplish anything. You are not just champions; you are pioneers of girls' rugby in Brynmawr."

Megan, as the team's captain, also spoke, reflecting on their incredible journey. "We started this journey as a group of girls with a dream," she said. "But we've become so much more than that. We've become a symbol of what can be achieved when individuals come together as a team and pursue their dreams with unwavering passion."

The celebration was a testament to the impact the Brynmawr Stars had made in their town and beyond. They had inspired other girls to take up rugby, showing them that they could achieve greatness in the sport. Their success had shattered stereotypes and opened doors for girls who aspired to play rugby.

In the days following their victory, the Brynmawr Stars received congratulatory messages and recognition from various quarters. The local newspaper featured them in a front-page article, lauding their journey from humble beginnings to regional champions. The town council honored them with a special reception, recognizing their contribution to the community.

Their success also had a profound effect on the boys' rugby teams at their school. The boys, who had once teased and doubted the girls, now viewed them as equals and friends. They offered to share the rugby field for practice sessions, fostering a sense of unity and camaraderie among the students.

The girls in their school who had initially doubted them had also changed their perspective. Many of them had attended the Brynmawr Stars' matches and had witnessed the team's determination and skill firsthand. They now looked up to Megan and her teammates as role models, and some of them even expressed an interest in joining the rugby team in the future.

The Brynmawr Stars were no longer just a girls' rugby team; they were a source of inspiration and pride for their town. They had become pioneers, breaking barriers and forging a path for future generations of girls who aspired to play rugby. They had shown that with determination, hard work, and unwavering belief, dreams could be realized.

As the weeks passed, the Brynmawr Stars continued to practice and play matches, but their journey had taken on a new dimension. They were no longer just focused on winning; they were focused on giving back to the community and inspiring others.

One day, Megan approached her teammates with an idea. "I think it's time we organize a rugby clinic for girls in our town," she said. "We can share our knowledge and skills, and encourage more girls to take up the sport."

The idea was met with enthusiastic approval from the team. They believed that it was their responsibility to pay forward the support and encouragement they had received. They wanted to create opportunities for other girls to discover the joys of rugby and experience the camaraderie of being part of a team.

With the help of Mrs. Evans and the support of their families, the Brynmawr Stars organized a girls' rugby clinic. They invited girls from their town to participate, regardless of their experience or skill level. The response was overwhelming, with girls of all ages eager to learn from the champions.

The clinic was a resounding success, with the Brynmawr Stars sharing their knowledge, skills, and passion for the sport. They taught the girls the basics of rugby, from passing and tackling to strategy and teamwork. The clinic was not just about physical skills; it was about instilling confidence, determination, and a sense of belonging.

The girls who attended the clinic left with a newfound enthusiasm for rugby and a sense of empowerment. They had seen firsthand what could be achieved when individuals came together as a team and pursued their dreams. The Brynmawr Stars had become their role models, their heroes, and their inspiration.

In addition to the clinic, the Brynmawr Stars also visited local schools to share their story and inspire other girls to pursue their passions. They emphasized the importance of hard work, determination, and self-belief in achieving one's goals. They encouraged girls to break free from stereotypes and pursue their dreams with unwavering passion.

Their impact extended beyond their town, as they received invitations to speak at regional events and sports conferences. They shared their journey, their challenges, and their triumphs, inspiring others to believe in the power of teamwork and perseverance.

One of the most touching moments came when Megan received a letter from a young girl named Sophie. Sophie had been following the Brynmawr Stars' journey from the beginning and had been inspired to join the girls' rugby team at her school. She expressed her gratitude to Megan and her teammates for showing her that girls could excel in rugby.

Moved by Sophie's letter, Megan and the team decided to pay her a surprise visit at her school. The moment they walked into the gymnasium where Sophie was practicing with her team, her face lit up with joy and disbelief. It was a moment that encapsulated the Brynmawr Stars' mission to inspire and empower others.

As the months passed, the Brynmawr Stars continued to practice and play matches, but their focus had shifted. They were no longer just champions on the field; they were champions of empowerment and inspiration. They had shown that girls could break barriers, shatter stereotypes, and achieve greatness in any field they chose.

Their journey had been one of resilience, determination, and unwavering belief in themselves. They had faced doubt, challenges, and adversity, but they had emerged victorious. They had not only reached for the stars; they had become stars, guiding others to follow their dreams and reach for their own stars.

The school recognized the Brynmawr Stars officially, celebrating their achievements and contributions to the community. The girls had not only excelled in rugby but had also become role models, mentors, and advocates for girls' empowerment.

As the years passed, the Brynmawr Stars pursued their individual paths, but their bond remained unbreakable. They continued to support each other in their endeavors, knowing that they had been part of something special, something that had changed their lives and the lives of others.

Megan, Amina, Lily, Amelia, Sarah, and the rest of the team had left an indelible mark on their town and the world of rugby. They had shown that with determination, hard work, and unwavering belief, dreams could be realized, barriers could be broken, and stars could shine brightly.

Their journey had been a testament to the power of teamwork, the strength of the human spirit, and the limitless possibilities that awaited those who dared to dream. The Brynmawr Stars had not only reached for the stars; they had become stars, illuminating the path for others to follow.

And as they looked up at the night sky, they knew that their light would continue to shine, guiding countless others to reach for their own stars and achieve their own dreams.

The End.

Under the Rugby Rainbow

Part 1

In the heart of the picturesque Yorkshire Dales, nestled among rolling green hills and quaint stone cottages, there lay a quiet village named Willowbrook. It was a place where life moved at a gentle pace, and where everyone knew their neighbors' names. It was in this tranquil village that lived a shy and introspective 10-year-old girl named Lucy.

Lucy was known for her shyness, a trait that often left her feeling like an outsider. She had a heart full of dreams and a mind brimming with curiosity, but when it came to making friends, her timidity held her back. She longed for the laughter and camaraderie she saw in other children, but the thought of initiating a conversation or joining in their games left her feeling anxious.

One crisp autumn day, as Lucy was walking home from school, she noticed a vibrant poster hanging on a community noticeboard. It caught her attention with its bold colors and exciting message. It was an advertisement for the formation of a girls' rugby team in Willowbrook.

Lucy had never considered playing rugby before. In fact, she had never played any organized sport. The idea of running, tackling, and being part of a team seemed both thrilling and terrifying. As she gazed at the poster, her heart fluttered with a mix of curiosity and nervousness.

That evening, Lucy sat at the kitchen table, fidgeting with her pencil and notebook. Her parents, Sarah and David, noticed her restlessness and exchanged knowing glances. They were aware of their daughter's struggle to make friends and were always on the lookout for opportunities to help her come out of her shell.

"Lucy," Sarah said gently, "what's on your mind, sweetheart?"

Lucy hesitated for a moment before finally speaking in a soft voice. "There's a girls' rugby team starting in Willowbrook, Mum. I saw a poster today."

David raised an intrigued eyebrow. "Rugby, huh? That's quite a sport. What do you think about it?"

Lucy looked down at her notebook, her fingers tracing the edges of the poster she had sketched. "I don't know, Dad. I'm not really good at making friends, and I'm not sure if I'd fit in with the other girls."

Her parents exchanged another knowing glance. They understood their daughter's concerns but also knew that stepping out of her comfort zone might be the key to helping her overcome her shyness.

Sarah leaned closer to Lucy and placed a reassuring hand on her shoulder. "Sweetie, sometimes trying something new can lead to wonderful surprises. You won't know until you give it a try. And remember, we'll be here to support you every step of the way."

David nodded in agreement. "Your mum's right, Lucy. Joining the rugby team could be a great opportunity to make new friends and discover new talents."

Lucy's heart swelled with gratitude for her parents' understanding and encouragement. Their unwavering support gave her the courage to consider taking the leap and exploring this unfamiliar world of rugby.

As the days passed, Lucy couldn't shake the thought of the girls' rugby team from her mind. She knew that attending a training session was the first step, but the idea of stepping onto a rugby pitch with girls she didn't know left her with butterflies in her stomach.

Finally, one crisp Saturday morning, after a hearty breakfast and a pep talk from her parents, Lucy decided to take the leap. Dressed in a pair of comfortable leggings and a t-shirt, she grabbed her worn-out sneakers and made her way to the village rugby field.

The field was alive with activity as boys and girls of various ages practiced their rugby skills. The air was filled with laughter, shouts, and the thud of rugby balls being passed and kicked. Lucy stood at the edge of the field, her heart pounding in her chest as she watched the girls' team practice.

Coach Jenkins, a warm and encouraging figure with a shock of gray hair, noticed Lucy's hesitant presence. He approached her with a friendly smile and a twinkle in his eyes. "Hello there," he said kindly. "Are you here to join our girls' rugby team?"

Lucy nodded, her voice barely above a whisper. "Yes, I am."

Coach Jenkins' warm smile remained unchanged. "That's fantastic! We're always happy to welcome new members. What's your name?"

"Lucy," she replied, her nervousness still evident.

"Well, Lucy, I'm Coach Jenkins," he said, extending a welcoming hand. "You're in for a great time. Let's get you started with some basic drills."

Lucy hesitated for a moment, her shyness threatening to hold her back. But she remembered her parents' encouragement, and she firmly shook Coach Jenkins' hand. It was a small step, but it felt like a giant leap for her.

As Lucy joined the other girls on the pitch, she couldn't help but feel overwhelmed. They ran, passed, and tackled with confidence and skill. Their laughter and camaraderie filled the air, creating an atmosphere of belonging that Lucy had rarely experienced.

For the first session, Lucy mostly observed, trying to absorb the rules and techniques of the game. She felt like a fish out of water, but Coach Jenkins and the other girls made her feel welcome, patiently explaining the fundamentals and encouraging her to participate when she felt ready.

During a break in the practice, as Lucy sat on the grass, taking in the vibrant sights and sounds around her, another girl approached her. She had a friendly smile and a twinkle in her eyes that reminded Lucy of Coach Jenkins.

"Hey there," the girl said cheerfully. "I noticed you're new. I'm Jasmine."

Lucy smiled back, feeling a glimmer of hope. "Hi, Jasmine. I'm Lucy."

Jasmine plopped down beside Lucy and struck up a conversation. She had an outgoing and friendly nature that put Lucy at ease. They talked about their interests, their favorite books, and their dreams. It turned out that they had much in common.

As the practice resumed, Jasmine introduced Lucy to the rest of the team. The other girls were just as welcoming as Jasmine had been. They shared their own stories of how they had started playing rugby and the challenges they had overcome. Lucy began to feel a sense of belonging she had never known before.

As weeks turned into months, Lucy continued to attend the rugby training sessions. She participated in drills and games, slowly building her skills and confidence. She discovered a natural aptitude for rugby, particularly as a quick and agile winger.

Coach Jenkins, with his patient guidance and unwavering encouragement, recognized Lucy's potential. He worked with her individually, helping her refine her passes, tackles, and kicks. Lucy's progress was evident, and her self-esteem began to blossom both on and off the pitch.

Her parents, watching from the sidelines with pride, saw their once-shy daughter transform into a confident and determined young girl. They marveled at her newfound passion for rugby and the friendships she was forming with her teammates, especially Jasmine, who had become her closest friend.

One sunny afternoon, as the girls gathered for a practice session, Coach Jenkins announced an exciting piece of news. "Girls," he said with a grin, "we've been invited to play our first match against a neighboring village team. It's a chance for us to put our skills to the test and show what we're made of."

Lucy felt a mix of excitement and nerves at the prospect of her first rugby match. She had come a long way from the shy girl who had hesitated to join the team. Now, she was a valued member, contributing her skills and determination to the group.

As the match day approached, Lucy and her teammates trained with even greater intensity. They honed their strategies, improved their teamwork, and supported each other both on and off the pitch. The bond among the girls grew stronger, cementing their status as a close-knit team.

Finally, the day of the big match arrived. The village rugby field buzzed with anticipation as families and villagers gathered to watch the girls in action. Lucy could feel her heart racing as she donned her rugby jersey and stepped onto the field with her teammates.

The opposing team from the neighboring village was formidable, but the Willowbrook girls were undaunted. Coach Jenkins had instilled in them the values of determination, teamwork, and sportsmanship. They knew that winning wasn't everything; what mattered most was giving their best effort and supporting each other.

The match was intense from the start, with both teams displaying remarkable determination and skill. The Willowbrook girls relied on their strategic play and teamwork to counter their opponents' strength and speed. Lucy, playing as a winger, used her agility to make impressive runs down the field.

As the game progressed, Lucy overcame her initial fear and hesitance. She remembered the support of her family, the encouragement of Coach Jenkins, and the friendship of Jasmine and her teammates. With renewed confidence, she seized an opportunity and made a crucial try, diving over the try line to score.

The cheers of the crowd and the hugs from her teammates filled Lucy's heart with pride. Her try had contributed to their narrow victory, and the sense of achievement was immeasurable. It was a moment she would cherish forever.

After the match, the team gathered to celebrate their success. They laughed, shared stories, and congratulated each other on a game well played. Lucy realized that she was no longer the shy girl on the sidelines; she was a valued team member with newfound friends and a growing sense of self-assuredness.

As evening descended and the sun dipped below the horizon, a breathtaking sight appeared in the sky. A rainbow arched gracefully, its vibrant colors painting a radiant arc across the heavens. The girls, still in their rugby jerseys, gazed up at the rainbow in awe.

Lucy felt a profound sense of gratitude and wonder. The rainbow seemed to symbolize her own journey, a transformation from a shy, solitary girl to a confident and happy team player, surrounded by friends who had become like family. She knew that she had found her place under the rugby rainbow, and she was determined to keep shining brightly.

Part 2

Lucy had taken her first tentative steps into the world of rugby, and although her heart was filled with excitement, her mind was still a swirl of uncertainty. She had attended a few training sessions with the Willowbrook girls' rugby team, and each time brought a mixture of wonder and nervousness.

As the weeks passed, Lucy's family continued to be her unwavering support system. Sarah and David saw the transformation happening within their daughter and were filled with pride and joy. Lucy's newfound confidence and the friendships she was forming warmed their hearts.

One evening, after Lucy's training session, she sat with her parents at the kitchen table, sipping on mugs of hot chocolate. The sun had dipped below the hills, casting a warm, golden glow into the room.

Sarah leaned forward, her eyes sparkling with curiosity. "Lucy, tell us about your rugby practice today. How did it go?"

Lucy took a moment to collect her thoughts, a smile playing on her lips. "Well, Mum, today we worked on our tackling skills. Coach Jenkins taught us how to tackle safely and effectively. He said that rugby is not just about running and scoring tries; it's about teamwork and supporting each other."

David nodded in agreement. "That sounds like an important lesson, Lucy. Teamwork is what makes rugby such a special sport."

Lucy's eyes lit up as she continued. "Yes, Dad, and I learned that even though rugby can be tough, it's also a lot of fun. I used to be so scared of getting tackled, but now I know how to do it right. And you know what? I tackled Jasmine today during practice, and she said it was a great tackle!"

Sarah and David exchanged a proud glance, their daughter's enthusiasm contagious. "That's wonderful, Lucy," Sarah said. "It sounds like you're really coming into your own on the rugby field."

Lucy nodded, her heart brimming with gratitude. "I am, Mum. And I'm making friends too. Jasmine is so friendly and outgoing, and she introduced me to the rest of the team. They're all really nice, and I feel like I belong."

David spoke with a gentle smile. "We're so proud of you, Lucy. Stepping out of your comfort zone and trying something new takes a lot of courage, and you're doing it so well."

Encouraged by her parents' support, Lucy's determination to excel in rugby grew stronger with each passing day. She knew that she still had much to learn, but she was eager to face every challenge head-on. Rugby had become more than just a sport to her; it was a journey of self-discovery and friendship.

The following Saturday, Lucy eagerly made her way to the rugby field for another training session. The sun was shining brightly, casting long shadows across the field. She wore her rugby jersey with pride, the Willowbrook emblem emblazoned on the front.

As Lucy arrived, she noticed that Coach Jenkins was busy setting up cones and tackling pads. It seemed that today's practice would focus on improving their tackling skills further. Lucy's heart raced with a mix of excitement and anticipation.

The other girls began to gather on the field, chatting and laughing as they put on their rugby gear. Lucy joined them, greeted by smiles and friendly hellos. Jasmine, as always, was at her side, her infectious enthusiasm making Lucy feel at ease.

"Hey, Lucy!" Jasmine exclaimed. "I heard Coach Jenkins has some exciting tackling drills planned for today. I can't wait to see what we'll learn."

Lucy nodded, her nerves tingling with anticipation. "Me too, Jasmine. I want to get even better at tackling."

As the practice began, Coach Jenkins gathered the girls in a circle and explained the importance of safe and effective tackling in rugby. He emphasized that rugby was a physical sport but also one built on respect and sportsmanship. Tackling, when done correctly, was a crucial skill that ensured the safety of all players.

Lucy listened intently, absorbing every word. She was determined to learn and improve. Coach Jenkins then demonstrated the proper technique for tackling, using one of the tackling pads as an example. He showed them how to approach the target, wrap their arms securely around it, and drive with their legs to bring it to the ground safely.

The girls watched with rapt attention, their eyes fixed on Coach Jenkins's every move. Lucy studied the demonstration closely, visualizing herself performing the tackle with precision and confidence.

After the demonstration, it was time for the girls to practice tackling. They paired up, with one girl holding the tackling pad and the other taking the role of the tackler. Lucy found herself paired with Jasmine, and together they practiced the techniques they had just learned.

Jasmine held the tackling pad firmly, her eyes filled with trust and encouragement. "You can do this, Lucy," she said with a reassuring smile.

Lucy took a deep breath, her nerves still present but no longer paralyzing. She approached the tackling pad, remembering Coach Jenkins's instructions. As she made contact, she felt the satisfying thud of her shoulder hitting the pad. She wrapped her arms around it securely and drove with her legs, bringing it down to the ground.

A chorus of cheers and applause erupted from the other girls. Lucy's heart swelled with pride and relief. She had tackled successfully, and the support of her teammates made her feel like she was on top of the world.

Jasmine gave her a high-five, her eyes shining with pride. "That was amazing, Lucy! You're a natural."

Lucy blushed but couldn't help but smile. With each successful tackle, her confidence grew, and she began to believe in her own abilities. She no longer felt like the timid outsider looking in; she was an integral part of the team, contributing her skills and determination.

As the weeks went by, the girls continued to practice their rugby skills diligently. Lucy's progress was evident, and she started to develop her own style of play. Coach Jenkins noticed her aptitude for speed and agility and encouraged her to consider the position of a winger, a player known for their ability to make quick runs down the field.

Lucy embraced the idea, and with Coach Jenkins's guidance, she honed her skills as a winger. She practiced her sprints, evasive maneuvers, and ball-handling techniques. She loved the feeling of the wind rushing past her as she sprinted down the field, her heart pounding with exhilaration.

The girls' rugby team of Willowbrook became a close-knit group, a sisterhood bonded by their shared passion for rugby and their determination to excel. They supported each other through every challenge, celebrated each other's successes, and laughed together during their breaks.

One sunny afternoon, Coach Jenkins gathered the girls for an important announcement. "Girls," he began with a smile, "I have some exciting news. We've been invited to play our first official match against a neighboring village team. It's a chance for us to put our skills to the test and show what we're made of."

The news sent a ripple of excitement through the team. The prospect of a real match, where they would compete as a team, was both thrilling and nerve-wracking. Lucy's heart raced at the thought of representing Willowbrook on the rugby field.

Coach Jenkins continued, "Remember, winning is not the only goal. What matters most is that you give your best effort and support each other, both on and off the field. You've come a long way, and I believe in each and every one of you."

Lucy nodded in agreement, her determination burning bright. She knew that the upcoming match would be a test of their teamwork, skills, and sportsmanship. She was ready to give it her all, not only for herself but for her newfound friends and the sport she had come to love.

The days leading up to the match were filled with intense training sessions, strategic planning, and the unwavering support of their families and the Willowbrook community. Lucy's parents, Sarah and David, watched with pride as their daughter prepared for the big day, her transformation from a shy girl to a confident rugby player nothing short of remarkable.

On the morning of the match, the village rugby field buzzed with excitement. Families, friends, and villagers gathered to support the Willowbrook girls' rugby team. The sun shone brightly in the sky, casting a warm glow over the field.

Lucy, wearing her rugby jersey with the number 11 on the back, stood alongside her teammates, their faces a mix of nerves and determination. Jasmine, who would be playing as a scrum-half, gave Lucy an encouraging smile. "We've got this, Lucy. Remember everything we've learned."

Lucy nodded, her heart filled with gratitude for her supportive friend. As the match began, she felt a surge of adrenaline and excitement. The opposing team from the neighboring village was formidable, their reputation as skilled rugby players well-known.

The first half of the match was intense, with both teams displaying remarkable determination and skill. The Willowbrook girls relied on their strategic play and teamwork to counter their opponents' strength and speed. Lucy, in her position as a winger, used her agility to make impressive runs down the field, dodging tackles and making passes.

The crowd cheered with every tackle, pass, and try, their voices a chorus of support for the young Willowbrook team. Lucy could hear her parents' encouraging shouts from the sidelines, and it gave her an extra burst of energy.

As the match progressed, Lucy's initial nervousness began to fade. She remembered the support of her family, the guidance of Coach Jenkins, and the unwavering friendship of Jasmine and her teammates. With each passing minute, she felt more like a member of a united team, determined to give their best effort.

In the closing minutes of the match, with the score tied, the Willowbrook girls launched a strategic play. Jasmine, the scrum-half, passed the ball to Lucy, who sprinted down the wing with all her might. The opposing team's defenders closed in, but Lucy used her agility to evade them.

With a burst of speed, Lucy reached the try line and dived over, scoring a crucial try for her team. The crowd erupted in cheers, and her teammates rushed to congratulate her. It was a moment of triumph, a testament to their hard work and dedication.

The final whistle blew, and the scoreboard showed a narrow victory for the Willowbrook girls. They had won their first official match, and the sense of accomplishment was palpable. Lucy's heart swelled with pride, not only for her try but for the entire team's performance.

After the match, the girls gathered on the field, their faces flushed with exertion and elation. Coach Jenkins approached them with a beaming smile. "Girls, that was an outstanding performance today. I'm so proud of each and every one of you. Remember, rugby is not just about winning; it's about playing with heart and supporting each other. You've shown that in spades."

Lucy nodded, her eyes shining with gratitude. She knew that rugby had become more than just a sport to her; it was a journey of self-discovery, friendship, and personal growth. She had learned that with determination, support, and a little courage, she could achieve great things.

As the girls celebrated their victory, Lucy realized that she was no longer the shy girl on the sidelines, watching others from a distance. She was an integral part of a team, a team that had not only won their first match but had also won a place in her heart.

As evening descended and the sky transformed into shades of orange and pink, a breathtaking sight appeared overhead. A rainbow arched gracefully, its vibrant colors painting a radiant arc across the heavens. The girls, still in their rugby jerseys, gazed up at the rainbow in awe.

Part 3

After the exhilaration of their first official match, the Willowbrook girls' rugby team found themselves buzzing with excitement and a renewed sense of purpose. Victory had given them a taste of what they were capable of, and they were hungry for more.

The day after the match, Lucy, Jasmine, and the rest of the team returned to their usual training routine. Coach Jenkins, with his ever-present smile, reminded them that success on the rugby field required hard work, dedication, and a commitment to continuous improvement.

As Lucy sprinted down the field during one of their drills, her heart felt lighter than it had in a long time. She reveled in the thrill of the wind rushing past her, the grass beneath her cleats, and the camaraderie of her teammates. Rugby had become her sanctuary, a place where she could be herself without the burden of shyness.

After practice, as Lucy and Jasmine sat on the grass, catching their breath, Lucy turned to her friend with a grateful smile. "Jasmine, I can't believe how much my life has changed since I joined the rugby team. I'm so thankful for all of you."

Jasmine beamed back at Lucy. "I feel the same way, Lucy. I used to be the only girl who played rugby in Willowbrook, and it was tough. But now, with all of you, it feels like I'm part of something special. We're a team, and we're doing something incredible together."

Lucy nodded in agreement. "You know, I used to be so shy, and making friends was really hard for me. But you, Jasmine, and the rest of the team have been so welcoming. I finally feel like I belong."

Jasmine's eyes sparkled with understanding. "Lucy, you belong here just as much as any of us. You've got amazing talent, and your determination is inspiring. I'm proud to call you my friend."

The words warmed Lucy's heart, and she realized how fortunate she was to have met Jasmine. Their friendship had been a guiding light, helping Lucy navigate the challenges of rugby and providing the support she needed to grow both as a player and as a person.

As the weeks went by, Lucy and Jasmine's friendship deepened. They spent their weekends practicing together, watching rugby matches on television, and even visiting the local library to read books about famous rugby players and the history of the sport. Lucy's passion for rugby was infectious, and Jasmine loved every moment of their rugby adventures.

One sunny Saturday, Lucy and Jasmine decided to take their rugby practice to a nearby park. They packed their rugby balls, cones, and tackling pads into a bag and set off on their bikes.

The park had a large open field with plenty of space for them to practice their drills and passes.

As they arrived at the park, they noticed a group of children playing soccer on one side of the field. Lucy and Jasmine found an empty space and began to set up their makeshift training ground. They laid out the cones, placed the tackling pad in position, and took a few practice passes.

Lucy couldn't help but feel a twinge of self-consciousness as she glanced over at the soccer players. They looked so confident and skilled, their laughter ringing out across the field. She wondered if they were as passionate about their sport as she was about rugby.

Jasmine noticed Lucy's hesitation and gave her a reassuring smile. "Don't worry, Lucy. We've got our own thing going here. Let's focus on our drills and have some fun."

Lucy nodded, grateful for Jasmine's support. They began their practice, working on passing, tackling, and evasive maneuvers. Their concentration was unwavering, and they were soon lost in the rhythm of their training.

As they practiced, the soccer players on the other side of the field began to take notice. A few of the children wandered over to watch, their curiosity piqued by the unusual sight of girls practicing rugby. They stood at a distance, whispering and pointing.

Lucy and Jasmine continued their drills, their movements fluid and precise. They were in sync, each pass and tackle executed with precision. The soccer players watched in fascination, their initial skepticism giving way to admiration.

One of the soccer players, a boy with curly hair and a friendly grin, approached the girls. "Hey," he called out, "that's some impressive stuff you're doing. Can I join in?"

Lucy and Jasmine exchanged surprised glances, then smiled at the boy. "Sure," Lucy replied, "the more, the merrier. What's your name?"

The boy introduced himself as Daniel and joined them in their drills. It turned out that he was a soccer enthusiast and had never played rugby before. However, he was eager to learn and excited to try something new.

Lucy and Jasmine patiently explained the basics of rugby to Daniel, from passing and tackling to the rules of the game. They demonstrated each technique and encouraged him to give it a try. Daniel was a quick learner, and his enthusiasm was contagious.

As they practiced together, Lucy, Jasmine, and Daniel found themselves forming an unexpected bond. Their shared love for sports transcended the boundaries of soccer and rugby. They laughed, exchanged stories, and encouraged each other to push their limits.

The soccer players who had been watching from a distance were soon drawn to the trio. They, too, wanted to give rugby a try. Lucy, Jasmine, and Daniel eagerly welcomed them into their impromptu training session. The park's open field buzzed with energy as children from different backgrounds and interests came together to learn and play.

After a few hours of practice and laughter, the group of children sat on the grass, catching their breath. They had discovered the joy of trying something new, making friends, and breaking down barriers between different sports and interests.

As they sat together, Lucy couldn't help but feel a sense of fulfillment. She had not only found her place within the rugby team but had also forged new friendships beyond the rugby pitch. The experience reinforced her belief that sports had the power to bring people together, regardless of their backgrounds or differences.

Over the following weeks, Lucy, Jasmine, and Daniel continued to practice together at the park, their group expanding as more children joined in. They had become a close-knit community of sports enthusiasts, celebrating their shared passion for rugby and soccer.

One sunny afternoon, as Lucy, Jasmine, and Daniel sat on the grass, watching the other children practice, Lucy felt a profound sense of gratitude for the friendship and support she had found through rugby. She turned to her friends with a smile.

"You know," Lucy began, "I used to be the shyest person I knew. I had trouble making friends, and I often felt like an outsider. But rugby changed all that. It brought me to all of you, and I'm so thankful for that."

Jasmine nodded in agreement. "Rugby has brought us together, Lucy, and it's not just about playing a sport. It's about the friendships we've formed and the experiences we've shared."

Daniel chimed in, "I never thought I'd be playing rugby, but I'm loving every minute of it. And I'm grateful to have friends like you to share this journey with."

As the sun began to dip below the horizon, casting a warm, golden glow over the park, Lucy realized that her life had taken a beautiful turn. Rugby had not only given her the confidence to be herself but had also opened the door to new friendships and unexpected adventures.

The rainbow of friendship had expanded beyond the rugby pitch, encompassing a diverse group of children brought together by their shared love for sports and their willingness to embrace the unknown. Lucy knew that she was no longer the shy girl who had once hesitated to make friends; she was a member of a vibrant and supportive community that celebrated individuality and camaraderie.

As Lucy, Jasmine, and Daniel watched the sun's last rays disappear, a feeling of contentment washed over them. They had discovered the magic of friendship under the rugby rainbow, and they were determined to cherish it for years to come.

Part 4

As the seasons changed and the days grew longer, Lucy's passion for rugby continued to burn brightly. The Willowbrook girls' rugby team had become an integral part of her life, and her transformation from a shy, reserved girl to a confident rugby player was nothing short of remarkable.

The support and camaraderie of her teammates, especially her dear friend Jasmine, had played a significant role in Lucy's growth. She felt like she was part of a close-knit family that celebrated each other's successes and supported one another through every challenge.

One sunny afternoon, Lucy and Jasmine sat on the grass after a rigorous training session. The field was alive with the sounds of children practicing various sports, and the warm breeze carried the scent of freshly mown grass.

Lucy turned to Jasmine with a thoughtful expression. "You know, Jasmine, I've been thinking. Rugby has given me so much, and I want to give back to the team in any way I can. I just don't know how."

Jasmine smiled warmly at her friend. "Lucy, you've already given so much to the team through your dedication and determination. But if you want to do more, there are plenty of ways. You could help organize team events, support our newer players, or even assist Coach Jenkins during training sessions."

Lucy nodded, her mind racing with possibilities. She was determined to contribute to the team's success and create a supportive environment for all its members.

As the weeks passed, Lucy took on the role of team organizer with enthusiasm. She helped plan team-building events, fundraisers, and community outreach activities. The girls' rugby team of Willowbrook became not just a sports team but a close-knit community that made a positive impact on their town.

One of Lucy's proudest moments came when she and Jasmine organized a rugby workshop for young girls in Willowbrook who were interested in learning the sport. They reached out to local schools and community centers, inviting girls of all ages to participate.

On the day of the workshop, the rugby field was buzzing with excitement. Lucy, Jasmine, and the rest of the team welcomed the eager young participants, their faces lit up with anticipation. It was a heartwarming sight, seeing girls from different backgrounds coming together to learn and play rugby.

Lucy and Jasmine led the workshop with confidence, sharing their knowledge and love for the sport. They taught the basics of passing, tackling, and teamwork, emphasizing the values of sportsmanship and camaraderie that were at the core of rugby.

The young girls listened intently, their eyes shining with enthusiasm. Lucy noticed one girl in particular, a shy 8-year-old named Emily, who seemed hesitant to join the activities. Lucy approached her with a warm smile.

"Hey there, Emily," Lucy said gently, "don't be shy. We're all here to have fun and learn together. Would you like to give it a try?"

Emily looked up at Lucy with a mixture of apprehension and curiosity. With a nod, she joined the group, slowly building her confidence with each pass and tackle. Lucy and Jasmine made sure to encourage and support her every step of the way.

As the workshop continued, Emily's shyness began to fade, replaced by a growing sense of accomplishment. She made her first successful pass and tackled a tackling pad with determination. Lucy watched with pride as Emily's smile grew wider with each achievement.

At the end of the workshop, as the young girls and their families gathered for a closing ceremony, Lucy and Jasmine presented each participant with a small rugby ball and a certificate of participation. Emily clutched her rugby ball tightly, her eyes filled with a sense of pride and belonging.

Lucy couldn't help but feel a deep sense of satisfaction as she looked at the smiling faces around her. She knew that rugby had the power to bring people together, to break down barriers, and to empower young girls like Emily to discover their own strengths.

As the days turned into weeks, Lucy's skills as a rugby player continued to improve. Coach Jenkins had recognized her natural aptitude for the game, particularly as a winger. Her speed, agility, and quick decision-making made her a valuable asset to the team.

During one training session, Coach Jenkins approached Lucy with a twinkle in his eye. "Lucy," he began, "I've been watching your progress, and I believe you have the potential to become an exceptional winger. You have a natural talent for reading the game and making quick decisions on the field."

Lucy's heart swelled with pride and gratitude. She had never imagined that she would receive such praise from her coach. "Thank you, Coach," she replied earnestly. "I'm willing to work hard and do my best for the team."

Coach Jenkins nodded. "That's the spirit, Lucy. Remember, rugby is not just about individual skill; it's about teamwork and supporting your teammates. Your abilities as a winger can make a significant difference in our games, but it's the unity of the team that will lead us to victory."

Lucy took Coach Jenkins's words to heart. She continued to train diligently, honing her skills as a winger and working on her passing, evasive maneuvers, and ball-handling techniques. She also sought guidance from her teammates, learning from their experiences and incorporating their advice into her game.

As the rugby season progressed, the Willowbrook girls' team faced increasingly challenging opponents. Each match tested their skills, determination, and teamwork. Lucy's role as a winger became crucial in creating scoring opportunities and defending against the opposing teams.

During a particularly intense match against a rival team, Lucy found herself in a pivotal moment. The score was tied, and the clock was ticking down. The Willowbrook girls were determined to secure a victory on their home turf.

With the ball in her hands, Lucy sprinted down the wing, dodging tackles and weaving through the opposing players. She could feel the eyes of her teammates and the crowd on her, but she remained focused on the task at hand. The try line was within reach, and she knew that this was her moment.

As she approached the try line, Lucy made a split-second decision. Instead of attempting to score the try herself, she passed the ball to a teammate who was in a better position to cross the line. The crowd held its breath as the teammate dove over the try line, scoring the winning try just as the final whistle blew.

The cheers from the crowd were deafening, and Lucy's teammates rushed to congratulate her. It was a selfless and strategic play that showcased Lucy's growth as a rugby player and her commitment to the team's success.

Coach Jenkins, watching from the sideline, couldn't have been prouder. He knew that Lucy's decision had not only secured a victory but had also reinforced the values of teamwork and selflessness that were at the heart of rugby.

After the match, Lucy and her teammates celebrated their hard-fought victory. Lucy's heart swelled with pride, not only for her role in the winning play but for the unity and determination of the entire team. They had overcome challenges, learned from each other, and grown stronger together.

As Lucy reflected on her journey, she realized that rugby had given her more than just a love for the sport. It had given her a sense of purpose, a community of friends, and the opportunity to discover her own talents and potential.

Under the rugby rainbow, Lucy had transformed from a shy, reserved girl into a confident and skilled rugby player. She knew that her journey was far from over and that the challenges and adventures that lay ahead would only strengthen her bond with her teammates and her love for the sport.

Part 5

As the rugby season progressed, the Willowbrook girls' rugby team continued to train tirelessly, honing their skills and strengthening their bonds of friendship. Their victories and challenges had shaped them into a formidable unit, and their determination remained unwavering.

Their efforts had not gone unnoticed, and they had garnered support from their school and community. The girls had become local heroes, inspiring other young girls to take up rugby and proving that they were just as capable as their male counterparts.

One sunny morning, during a team training session, Coach Jenkins gathered the girls together for an important announcement. His face held a mixture of pride and anticipation. "Girls," he began, "I have some exciting news. We've been invited to participate in a regional rugby tournament next month."

The girls exchanged excited glances, their hearts filled with anticipation. A regional tournament was a significant opportunity to showcase their skills and compete against highly skilled teams from neighboring towns.

Lucy's eyes sparkled with enthusiasm as she listened to Coach Jenkins. She knew that this tournament would be their biggest challenge yet, but she was eager to take it on with her teammates by her side.

Coach Jenkins continued, "This tournament will test us in ways we haven't been tested before. We'll be facing seasoned teams with years of experience. But I have complete faith in each one of you. We've trained hard, we've grown as a team, and we're ready to give it our all."

Lucy nodded in agreement, her heart filled with determination. The regional tournament would be a chance to prove themselves on a larger stage, to demonstrate the values of teamwork and sportsmanship that rugby stood for, and to inspire even more young girls to take up the sport.

In the weeks leading up to the tournament, the Willowbrook girls dedicated themselves to rigorous training and preparation. They focused on refining their plays, perfecting their passes, and working on their defensive strategies. Their unity as a team grew stronger with each passing day.

The tournament day arrived with a sense of excitement and nervous anticipation. The Willowbrook girls, in their blue and white jerseys, gathered at the rugby field, their faces reflecting a mix of determination and camaraderie. Their families and supporters had turned out in full force, their cheers echoing across the field.

Their first match was against a team from a neighboring town, a formidable opponent with a reputation for strong defense and skilled players. The match promised to be a test of the Willowbrook girls' abilities and teamwork.

As the referee's whistle signaled the start of the match, Lucy felt a surge of adrenaline. The opposing team was fast and aggressive, their tackles fierce and determined. The Willowbrook girls found themselves in a fierce battle, defending their try line with unwavering resolve.

Lucy, as a winger, used her speed and agility to make strategic runs down the field, dodging tackles and making crucial passes to her teammates. She could feel the weight of the match on her shoulders, but she knew she was not alone. Her teammates were by her side, supporting and encouraging each other.

The first half of the match was intense, with both teams giving their all. The score remained tied, and the crowd watched with bated breath as the girls displayed their skills and determination. Lucy's parents, Sarah and David, cheered from the sidelines, their hearts filled with pride for their daughter's dedication and growth.

During a brief break between halves, Coach Jenkins gathered the girls together. "You're doing great out there," he said with a reassuring smile. "Remember, this is a team effort. Keep communicating, support each other, and trust in your training. We can win this."

The Willowbrook girls nodded in agreement, their determination renewed. They returned to the field for the second half with a renewed sense of purpose, their eyes fixed on the prize.

As the match continued, Lucy and her teammates pushed themselves to their limits. They executed intricate plays, defended their try line with tenacity, and tackled with precision. The opposing team, equally determined, fought back with equal vigor.

In the closing minutes of the match, with the score still tied, the Willowbrook girls found themselves in a crucial position. Lucy, with the ball in her hands, made a daring run down the wing, evading tackles and sprinting toward the try line. The opposing team's defenders closed in, their determination matching Lucy's speed.

In a split-second decision, Lucy made a precise pass to her teammate, Emily, who was in the perfect position to score. With a burst of energy, Emily sprinted across the try line, scoring the winning try for Willowbrook.

The crowd erupted in cheers, and Lucy's teammates rushed to congratulate her and Emily. It was a moment of triumph, a testament to their teamwork, determination, and the values they had learned through rugby.

The victory in their first match gave the Willowbrook girls a surge of confidence as they headed into the tournament's subsequent rounds. Match after match, they displayed their skills and resilience, surprising everyone with their ability to hold their own against experienced teams.

Lucy's role as a winger became increasingly crucial, as she continued to make strategic runs, set up scoring opportunities, and defend with unwavering determination. Her confidence had grown immensely since the early days of her rugby journey, and she knew that she had found her place on the team.

As the tournament progressed, the Willowbrook girls faced a series of nail-biting matches, each one more challenging than the last. Their victories and defeats were met with grace and sportsmanship, and they earned the respect of their opponents and the admiration of the crowd.

Finally, they found themselves in the tournament final, a high-stakes match against a seasoned team that had dominated the regional rugby scene for years. The Willowbrook girls were the underdogs, facing a formidable opponent on the grand stage.

The atmosphere was electric as the final match began. The crowd watched with anticipation, knowing that they were witnessing a historic moment for the Willowbrook girls' rugby team. Lucy and her teammates were determined to give it their all, to prove that they were a force to be reckoned with.

The match was a fierce battle, with both teams displaying exceptional skill and determination. Lucy's heart pounded as she made strategic runs, her body aching from the intensity of the game. She knew that this was the moment they had trained for, the chance to show the world what they were capable of.

In the closing minutes of the match, with the score tied, Lucy found herself in possession of the ball. The opposing team's defenders closed in, their tackles relentless. Lucy knew that she had to make a decision, and she had to make it quickly.

With a burst of speed and a strategic sidestep, Lucy evaded the defenders and sprinted toward the try line. She could hear the roar of the crowd, the cheers of her teammates, and the pounding of her heart in her chest.

As she reached the try line, Lucy made a split-second decision. Instead of attempting to score the try herself, she passed the ball to her teammate, Sarah, who was in a better position to cross the line. Sarah seized the opportunity and dove over the try line, scoring the winning try.

The crowd erupted in cheers, and Lucy's teammates rushed to embrace her and Sarah. It was a moment of triumph, a culmination of months of hard work, dedication, and unwavering teamwork.

The Willowbrook girls had won the regional tournament, proving that they were a force to be reckoned with in the world of rugby. Their victory was a testament to their passion, determination, and the values of unity and sportsmanship that they had embraced.

As they celebrated their victory, Lucy couldn't help but feel a profound sense of gratitude for her teammates, her coach, and the sport of rugby itself. It had brought her out of her shell, forged deep friendships, and given her the confidence to pursue her dreams.

The story of the Willowbrook girls' rugby team was one of triumph and perseverance, a testament to the power of teamwork and the belief that anyone, regardless of their background or circumstances, could achieve greatness through dedication and unity.

Under the rugby rainbow, Lucy and her teammates had discovered the true meaning of sportsmanship, friendship, and the limitless potential that lay within each of them. The victory in the regional tournament was just the beginning of their journey, a journey filled with possibilities, challenges, and the unwavering support of their teammates and community.

The rainbow of their success stretched far beyond the rugby field, a symbol of their shared dreams and the bonds that held them together. The Willowbrook girls knew that they had not only won a tournament but had also won the hearts of everyone who had witnessed their remarkable journey.

Part 6

The days leading up to the regional rugby tournament were filled with excitement and anticipation in Willowbrook. The girls' rugby team had earned their spot in the competition through hard work, dedication, and a series of impressive victories. Their journey from a group of diverse, inexperienced girls to a united and skilled team had captured the hearts of the entire town.

Coach Jenkins had intensified their training regimen in preparation for the regional tournament. The girls practiced tirelessly, refining their plays, perfecting their passes, and working on their fitness. Every member of the team felt a sense of responsibility and commitment, not just to themselves but to each other.

Lucy, in particular, had grown immensely as a rugby player. Her natural talent as a winger, combined with her determination and improved skills, made her a formidable force on the field. She had learned to read the game, make split-second decisions, and communicate effectively with her teammates.

As the day of the tournament approached, Lucy couldn't help but feel a mixture of nerves and excitement. The regional tournament would be their biggest challenge yet, with highly skilled teams from neighboring towns and communities. It was an opportunity to showcase their abilities and the values of teamwork and sportsmanship they had embraced.

On the morning of the tournament, the Willowbrook girls gathered at the rugby field, their faces reflecting a mix of determination and camaraderie. Their blue and white jerseys bore the emblem of a willow tree, a symbol of their town's spirit and resilience.

The families and supporters had turned out in full force, their cheers and applause filling the air with encouragement. Lucy's parents, Sarah and David, stood proudly among the spectators, their hearts filled with pride for their daughter and her teammates.

Their first match of the tournament was against a team from a neighboring town known for their strong defense and skilled players. The atmosphere was charged with anticipation as the referee's whistle signaled the start of the match.

Lucy felt a surge of adrenaline as she lined up on the wing, her cleats digging into the grass. The opposing team was fast and aggressive, their tackles fierce and determined. It was clear from the start that this match would be a fierce battle.

The first half of the match was intense, with both teams giving their all. The score remained tied, and the crowd watched with bated breath as the girls displayed their skills and determination. Lucy's parents, along with the rest of the spectators, were on the edge of their seats, absorbed in the thrilling contest.

During a brief break between halves, Coach Jenkins gathered the girls together. His words were a source of inspiration and motivation. "You're doing great out there," he said with a reassuring smile. "Remember, this is a team effort. Keep communicating, support each other, and trust in your training. We can win this."

The Willowbrook girls nodded in agreement, their determination renewed. They returned to the field for the second half with a renewed sense of purpose, their eyes fixed on the prize.

As the match continued, Lucy and her teammates pushed themselves to their limits. They executed intricate plays, defended their try line with tenacity, and tackled with precision. The opposing team, equally determined, fought back with equal vigor.

In the closing minutes of the match, with the score still tied, the Willowbrook girls found themselves in a crucial position. Lucy, with the ball in her hands, made a daring run down the wing, evading tackles and sprinting toward the try line. The opposing team's defenders closed in, their determination matching Lucy's speed.

In a split-second decision, Lucy made a precise pass to her teammate, Emily, who was in the perfect position to score. Emily seized the opportunity and dove over the try line, scoring the winning try for Willowbrook.

The crowd erupted in cheers, and Lucy's teammates rushed to congratulate her and Emily. It was a moment of triumph, a testament to their teamwork, determination, and the values they had learned through rugby.

The victory in their first match gave the Willowbrook girls a surge of confidence as they headed into the tournament's subsequent rounds. Match after match, they displayed their skills and resilience, surprising everyone with their ability to hold their own against experienced teams.

Lucy's role as a winger became increasingly crucial, as she continued to make strategic runs, set up scoring opportunities, and defend with unwavering determination. Her confidence had grown immensely since the early days of her rugby journey, and she knew that she had found her place on the team.

As the tournament progressed, the Willowbrook girls faced a series of nail-biting matches, each one more challenging than the last. Their victories and defeats were met with grace and sportsmanship, and they earned the respect of their opponents and the admiration of the crowd.

Finally, they found themselves in the tournament final, a high-stakes match against a seasoned team that had dominated the regional rugby scene for years. The Willowbrook girls were the underdogs, facing a formidable opponent on the grand stage.

The atmosphere was electric as the final match began. The crowd watched with anticipation, knowing that they were witnessing a historic moment for the Willowbrook girls' rugby team. Lucy and her teammates were determined to give it their all, to prove that they were a force to be reckoned with.

The match was a fierce battle, with both teams displaying exceptional skill and determination. Lucy's heart pounded as she made strategic runs, her body aching from the intensity of the game. She knew that this was the moment they had trained for, the chance to show the world what they were capable of.

In the closing minutes of the match, with the score tied, Lucy found herself in possession of the ball. The opposing team's defenders closed in, their tackles relentless. Lucy knew that she had to make a decision, and she had to make it quickly.

With a burst of speed and a strategic sidestep, Lucy evaded the defenders and sprinted toward the try line. She could hear the roar of the crowd, the cheers of her teammates, and the pounding of her heart in her chest.

As she reached the try line, Lucy made a split-second decision. Instead of attempting to score the try herself, she passed the ball to her teammate, Sarah, who was in a better position to cross the line. Sarah seized the opportunity and dove over the try line, scoring the winning try.

The crowd erupted in cheers, and Lucy's teammates rushed to embrace her and Sarah. It was a moment of triumph, a culmination of months of hard work, dedication, and unwavering teamwork.

The Willowbrook girls had won the regional tournament, proving that they were a force to be reckoned with in the world of rugby. Their victory was a testament to their passion, determination, and the values of unity and sportsmanship that they had embraced.

As they celebrated their victory, Lucy couldn't help but feel a profound sense of gratitude for her teammates, her coach, and the sport of rugby itself. It had brought her out of her shell, forged deep friendships, and given her the confidence to pursue her dreams.

The story of the Willowbrook girls' rugby team was one of triumph and perseverance, a testament to the power of teamwork and the belief that anyone, regardless of their background or circumstances, could achieve greatness through dedication and unity.

Under the rugby rainbow, Lucy and her teammates had discovered the true meaning of sportsmanship, friendship, and the limitless potential that lay within each of them. The victory in the regional tournament was just the beginning of their journey, a journey filled with possibilities, challenges, and the unwavering support of their teammates and community.

The rainbow of their success stretched far beyond the rugby field, a symbol of their shared dreams and the bonds that held them together. The Willowbrook girls knew that they had not only won a tournament but had also won the hearts of everyone who had witnessed their remarkable journey.

The End.

The Unstoppable Scrum

Part 1

In the picturesque town of St. Andrews nestled in the heart of Scotland, where the rugged coastline met rolling hills, there was a small but passionate community. It was a place where traditions ran deep, and among these traditions, rugby held a special place in the hearts of the townsfolk.

At St. Andrews Primary School, the boys' rugby team was renowned for their skill and dedication. The cheers of their supporters echoed through the town on match days, and their victories were celebrated with pride. But there was one thing missing – a girls' rugby team to share in the glory of the sport.

Fiona, a spirited 12-year-old with fiery red hair and a determined spirit, had long dreamt of playing rugby. She had grown up watching her brother and the other boys in the neighborhood play, and her heart yearned to be out there on the pitch, tackling, running, and scoring tries.

One sunny afternoon, after a spirited discussion with her friends at school, Fiona decided it was time to take action. She approached the school's sports coordinator, Mr. MacGregor, with a bold proposal.

"Mr. MacGregor," she began, her eyes shining with determination, "I think it's high time we had a girls' rugby team at St. Andrews Primary. There are plenty of girls who love the sport, and we deserve a chance to play just like the boys."

Mr. MacGregor, a kind-hearted man who had always admired Fiona's spirit, nodded thoughtfully. "You make a compelling case, Fiona. I'll speak to the school board and see what we can do about it."

Weeks passed, and Fiona's enthusiasm remained undiminished. She wore her rugby jersey to school every day, a visual testament to her commitment to the sport. And then, the news she had been waiting for arrived.

"We're going to have a girls' rugby team," Mr. MacGregor announced during assembly one bright morning. Fiona's heart soared, and the applause from her fellow students filled the hall.

The girls' rugby team at St. Andrews Primary was born. Fiona was appointed as the captain, a role she embraced with pride. But as the team started training and preparing for their first match, they soon realized they were facing a daunting challenge.

Their opponents were more experienced, with well-established girls' rugby teams from neighboring towns. The St. Andrews girls were passionate about the sport, but many of them were new to rugby, and their skills were far from advanced.

Fiona watched the other teams practice with a mixture of awe and determination. Their passes were crisp, their tackles fierce, and their strategies seemed almost mystical in their complexity. It was clear that if the St. Andrews girls were going to compete, they needed guidance and training from someone who understood the intricacies of the game.

One evening, after a particularly challenging training session, Fiona gathered her teammates in a circle on the field. The sun was setting, casting a warm, golden glow over the grass.

"Listen, girls," Fiona began, her voice filled with determination. "I know we're new to this, and it's going to be tough. But we have something they don't – heart and passion. We might not be the most skilled team right now, but we can work hard and improve. We can show everyone that we're a force to be reckoned with."

The girls nodded in agreement, their faces reflecting the same determination that burned in Fiona's eyes. They were in this together, and they were not going to back down from a challenge.

As the days turned into weeks, the St. Andrews girls' rugby team trained tirelessly, dedicating themselves to the sport. But they couldn't help but feel that they were missing something – a guiding hand, someone who could help them unlock their potential and develop the skills and strategies needed to compete at a higher level.

Little did they know that their prayers were about to be answered in the form of a new coach who would change their lives and their approach to rugby forever.

Part 2

The St. Andrews Primary School girls' rugby team had shown immense determination and passion on the field, but they were facing a steep learning curve. Their opponents in the upcoming matches were seasoned teams with years of experience. Fiona, their spirited captain, knew that they needed more than just heart to succeed.

It was on a rainy afternoon, while the girls were practicing on the muddy rugby pitch, that something unexpected happened. As they struggled with their passes and tackles, a tall figure in a raincoat and well-worn rugby boots appeared on the sideline, observing their efforts.

Fiona squinted through the rain, trying to make out the newcomer's face. The stranger's presence seemed out of place on this dreary day.

The coach, Mr. MacGregor, approached the mysterious figure. "Can I help you?" he asked, his voice carrying a tone of curiosity.

The stranger pulled back the hood of the raincoat, revealing a face that was weathered and wise, with a knowing smile. "I heard you've got a girls' rugby team," she said. "And it seems like they could use a bit of guidance."

Fiona watched in astonishment as the stranger stepped onto the field. She had the presence of someone who had spent a lifetime on rugby pitches.

Mr. MacGregor, recognizing the opportunity that had just presented itself, welcomed the newcomer. "I'm Mr. MacGregor, the school's sports coordinator. We would be grateful for any help you can offer."

The stranger extended her hand with a warm smile. "I'm Coach Thompson. I used to play professionally, and I've been looking for a way to give back to the sport that has given me so much."

Fiona's eyes widened in disbelief. Coach Thompson was a former professional rugby player, a legend in her own right. She had seen her play on television and admired her skills.

With Coach Thompson on board, the St. Andrews girls' rugby team's training took on a new dimension. She brought innovative ideas and a wealth of experience that quickly earned her the respect and admiration of the team.

Their first practice session under Coach Thompson's guidance was eye-opening. She emphasized the importance of teamwork, strategy, and communication above all else. While they ran drills and practiced their passes, she instilled in them the fundamental principles of rugby.

"Rugby is not just about individual talent," Coach Thompson explained. "It's about how well you work together as a team. The strongest player is only as strong as the weakest link."

Fiona absorbed Coach Thompson's words like a sponge. It was not just about running fast or tackling hard; it was about understanding the game, making split-second decisions, and supporting each other on the field.

As the weeks went by, Coach Thompson's impact on the team became evident. Fiona, with her sharp mind and natural leadership qualities, emerged as her most attentive student. She absorbed every piece of advice and tactical insight Coach Thompson shared, determined to lead her team to success.

The other girls, too, were improving by leaps and bounds. They learned the importance of positioning, passing under pressure, and reading the game. Coach Thompson was patient yet demanding, pushing them to their limits while instilling in them a deep love for the sport.

Off the field, the girls spent hours studying game footage, discussing strategies, and visualizing their plays. They had become a tight-knit unit, each member playing to her strengths and supporting her teammates. The camaraderie among them was palpable, a testament to their shared passion and their coach's guidance.

One evening, after a particularly intense training session, Coach Thompson gathered the team around her. The setting sun cast a warm glow over the rugby field.

"Girls, I've seen tremendous improvement in each one of you," Coach Thompson began. "But remember, it's not just about the skills you've learned. It's about how you apply them on the field. Rugby is a game of strategy and teamwork. The more you understand the game, the better you'll be at outsmarting your opponents."

Fiona nodded in agreement, her determination unwavering. She had not only improved her own skills but had also become a student of the game, absorbing every lesson Coach Thompson had to offer.

Coach Thompson continued, "In our next match, I want you to focus on applying the tactics we've learned. Remember your positions, communicate with your teammates, and trust in each other. That's how you'll become an unstoppable force on the field."

The girls nodded, their faces reflecting a mix of determination and excitement. With Coach Thompson's guidance, they felt ready to face their next challenge, armed not just with newfound skills but with a deeper understanding of the game.

As the days turned into weeks, the St. Andrews girls' rugby team underwent a transformation. They had evolved from a group of passionate but inexperienced players into a formidable unit with a deeper understanding of rugby's intricacies. Coach Thompson's influence had been nothing short of miraculous.

The town of St. Andrews took notice of the team's dedication and progress. The support from their families, schoolmates, and the community swelled with each passing day. The girls felt a sense of responsibility to live up to the expectations they had created.

Part 3

Under the guidance of Coach Thompson, the St. Andrews Primary School girls' rugby team was undergoing a remarkable transformation. Fiona, their determined captain, had absorbed every lesson like a sponge, and her keen rugby mind was constantly at work, dissecting plays, and strategizing.

The girls, too, had embraced the new approach to training with enthusiasm. They no longer just focused on running drills and practicing tackles; they delved into the intricacies of rugby, learning how to read the game and anticipate their opponents' moves.

Coach Thompson's training sessions were intense and demanding, but they were also filled with camaraderie and a deep love for the sport. She had instilled in the girls the importance of working as a cohesive unit, supporting each other both on and off the field.

As weeks turned into months, the girls' progress was evident. Their passes were crisper, their tackles more precise, and their understanding of the game continued to deepen. Coach Thompson had a knack for breaking down complex tactics into simple concepts, making it easier for the girls to grasp.

Fiona, in particular, had blossomed as a rugby player and a leader. She had always possessed a natural leadership quality, and under Coach Thompson's mentorship, she had refined her ability to inspire and guide her teammates. Her vision on the field had become a game-changer, allowing her to make quick decisions that often led to crucial plays.

One sunny afternoon, as the team practiced their lineouts, Fiona called for a huddle. She had something important to share with her teammates.

"Girls," Fiona began, her voice filled with determination, "we've come a long way since the beginning. Coach Thompson has taught us so much, and we've worked hard to improve our skills. But it's not just about individual growth; it's about becoming a cohesive team."

The girls nodded in agreement, their eyes fixed on Fiona. They respected her not just as their captain but as a player who had shown tremendous dedication and progress.

Fiona continued, "In our next match, I want us to focus on playing to our strengths. Coach Thompson has taught us to read the game, anticipate our opponents, and use our skills strategically. We're not just going to rely on brute force; we're going to outsmart our opponents."

The girls' faces reflected a mixture of determination and excitement. They had come to understand that rugby was not just about physicality; it was a mental game as well. With Coach

Thompson's guidance and Fiona's leadership, they felt more prepared than ever.

Their next few matches were a testament to their growth and progress. The St. Andrews girls had become a formidable team, employing the strategies and tactics they had learned from Coach Thompson.

Their passes were sharp, their communication on the field was seamless, and they moved as a unit, supporting each other in both attack and defense. Fiona's vision on the field was evident as she orchestrated plays that often left their opponents bewildered.

The St. Andrews girls started to win matches, a testament to their hard work, clever strategies, and unwavering teamwork. They earned a reputation for being the 'unstoppable scrum,' a team that couldn't be easily defeated.

Off the field, the support from their families, schoolmates, and the community grew stronger. The town of St. Andrews had embraced their girls' rugby team, and their matches were attended by enthusiastic crowds that cheered them on with fervor.

Coach Thompson watched with pride as the girls continued to excel. She knew that they had the potential to achieve greatness in rugby and beyond. But she also reminded them that their journey was just beginning, and there was much more to learn and achieve.

One crisp morning, as the girls gathered for practice, Coach Thompson had a surprise for them. She introduced a new set of drills that focused on teamwork, quick decision-making, and adaptability. The drills were challenging and required the girls to think on their feet, responding to changing situations on the field.

"We've come a long way, girls," Coach Thompson said, her eyes filled with pride. "But there's always room for improvement. These drills will push you to think creatively, adapt to different scenarios, and make quick decisions. Remember, rugby is a dynamic game, and the more you can anticipate and respond, the better you'll be."

The girls embraced the new drills with enthusiasm, relishing the opportunity to challenge themselves and further hone their skills. They understood that to truly become an unstoppable force on the rugby field, they needed to continue growing and learning.

As the weeks passed, the St. Andrews girls' rugby team continued to flourish under Coach Thompson's guidance. Their matches became showcases of clever strategies, precise execution, and unwavering teamwork.

Fiona, in particular, had become a master at reading the game. She could anticipate her opponents' moves, set up scoring opportunities for her teammates, and make split-second decisions that often turned the tide of a match in their favor.

Their victories drew the attention of not just their town but also neighboring communities. The St. Andrews girls were no longer just underdogs; they were a force to be reckoned with in the world of girls' rugby.

However, Coach Thompson reminded them that their journey was far from over. The ultimate test awaited them – a regional tournament where they would face the top teams in Scotland. It was a challenge that would push them to their limits and require them to apply everything they had learned under Coach Thompson's guidance.

As the day of the regional tournament approached, the St. Andrews girls felt a mixture of excitement and nerves. They knew that they were no longer just competing for themselves but for their town, their families, and the legacy they had built as the 'unstoppable scrum.'

Their skills, strategies, and teamwork would be put to the ultimate test, and they were determined to prove that even underdogs could rise to the top with hard work, dedication, and the right guidance. The regional tournament was their chance to shine, and they were ready to face it head-on, armed with the lessons they had learned and the unbreakable team spirit that had brought them this far.

Part 4

The day of the regional tournament had arrived, and a palpable sense of excitement and anticipation filled the air. The St. Andrews Primary School girls' rugby team, known throughout their town as the 'unstoppable scrum,' had come a long way since their humble beginnings.

As they boarded the bus that would take them to the tournament venue, Fiona, their determined captain, couldn't help but reflect on their journey. It had been a remarkable transformation, from a group of passionate but inexperienced players to a formidable team that was now ready to compete at a regional level.

Coach Thompson had been their guiding light, instilling in them the importance of strategy, teamwork, and mental agility. Their training had been intense, and their dedication unwavering. They had become a close-knit unit, each member playing to her strengths and supporting her teammates.

The journey to the tournament venue was filled with laughter and nervous excitement. The girls chatted animatedly, discussing their tactics and strategies for the matches ahead. They knew that the competition would be fierce, but they were ready to face the challenge head-on.

As they arrived at the tournament venue, they were greeted by a sea of rugby pitches, each one buzzing with activity. Teams from all over Scotland had gathered for the regional tournament, and the atmosphere was electric.

Coach Thompson gathered the St. Andrews girls in a circle for a final pep talk. "Remember everything we've worked on," she reminded them. "Focus on your positions, communicate with each other, and trust in your abilities. You've come a long way, and you're more than capable of competing at this level."

The girls nodded in agreement, their determination shining through. They had learned valuable lessons from Coach Thompson, and they were eager to put them into practice on the field.

Their first match of the tournament was against a well-established team from a neighboring town. The St. Andrews girls took to the field with a sense of purpose, their hearts pounding with anticipation.

From the very start, it was clear that this would be a closely contested match. The opposing team had experience on their side, but the St. Andrews girls had something equally valuable – a deep understanding of the game and an unbreakable team spirit.

The match was a thrilling display of rugby prowess. The St. Andrews girls employed the strategies and tactics they had learned from Coach Thompson. Their passes were precise, their tackles relentless, and their communication on the field was seamless.

Fiona, in her role as captain, orchestrated plays that often left their opponents scrambling to defend. Her ability to read the game and make quick decisions had become a key asset for the team.

As the match entered its final minutes, the score was tied. The tension on the field was palpable, and the crowd watched with bated breath. It was a defining moment for the St. Andrews girls, an opportunity to prove that they belonged among the top teams in Scotland.

In a crucial play, Fiona made a strategic call during a scrum. She signaled to her teammates, and they executed the play flawlessly. The opposing team was caught off guard, and the St. Andrews girls seized the opportunity.

With a burst of speed and a perfectly timed pass, they moved the ball swiftly down the field. Fiona, with determination in her eyes, sprinted toward the try line. She could hear the cheers of her teammates, the roar of the crowd, and the pounding of her heart in her chest.

As she reached the try line, Fiona made a split-second decision. Instead of attempting to score the try herself, she passed the ball to her teammate, Emma, who was in a better position to cross the line. Emma seized the opportunity and dove over the try line, scoring the winning try.

The crowd erupted in cheers, and the St. Andrews girls rushed to embrace Fiona and Emma. It was a moment of triumph, a culmination of months of hard work, dedication, and unwavering teamwork.

The victory in their first match sent a powerful message to the other teams in the tournament. The 'unstoppable scrum' was not to be underestimated. They had not only held their own against an experienced team but had emerged victorious.

As the tournament continued, the St. Andrews girls' confidence grew. They won match after match, employing the clever strategies and tactics they had learned from Coach Thompson. Their reputation as a formidable team continued to grow, and their matches were now a highlight of the tournament.

In the semifinals, they faced a team that had been a dominant force in girls' rugby for years. The odds were stacked against them, but the St. Andrews girls were undeterred. They knew that they had the skills, strategies, and teamwork to compete at the highest level.

The match was a fierce battle, with both teams displaying their best rugby. It was a showcase of talent and determination, with each try and tackle met with thunderous applause from the crowd.

As the final whistle blew, the scoreboard showed a narrow victory for the St. Andrews girls. It was a stunning upset, and their jubilant celebration echoed through the tournament venue.

They had advanced to the finals, where they would face their toughest opponent yet – a team that had won the regional tournament for several years running. The odds were against them, but the 'unstoppable scrum' was not one to back down from a challenge.

In the days leading up to the finals, the St. Andrews girls practiced tirelessly. They analyzed their opponent's playing style, devised new strategies, and honed their skills. Coach Thompson reminded them that this was their chance to make history, to prove that hard work and determination could overcome even the most formidable opponents.

The day of the finals arrived, and the atmosphere at the tournament venue was electric. The crowd had gathered in anticipation of an epic showdown between the reigning champions and the underdog St. Andrews girls.

As the teams took the field, Fiona looked around at her teammates. They were no longer just a group of girls who loved rugby; they were a family bound by their shared passion and their journey of growth and transformation.

The final match was a nail-biting contest, with both teams displaying their best rugby. The reigning champions were a formidable force, with years of experience and a reputation for dominance.

The St. Andrews girls, however, were not intimidated. They played with a fierce determination, executing the strategies and tactics they had learned from Coach Thompson. The match was a showcase of clever plays, precise passes, and unrelenting defense.

As the game reached its final moments, the score was tied. The tension on the field was palpable, and the crowd watched with bated breath. It was a moment that would define the St. Andrews girls' journey – a chance to prove that with teamwork and smart play, even underdogs could rise to the top.

In a heart-pounding sequence of plays, the St. Andrews girls found themselves in possession of the ball. The opposing team's defenders closed in, their tackles relentless. Fiona knew that she had to make a decision, and she had to make it quickly.

With a burst of speed and a strategic sidestep, Fiona evaded the defenders and sprinted toward the try line. She could hear the roar of the crowd, the cheers of her teammates, and the pounding of her heart in her chest.

As she reached the try line, Fiona made a split-second decision. Instead of attempting to score the try herself, she passed the ball to her teammate, Emma, who was in a better position to cross the line. Emma seized the opportunity and dove over the try line, scoring the winning try.

The crowd erupted in cheers, and the St. Andrews girls rushed to embrace Fiona and Emma. It was a moment of triumph, a testament to their hard work, clever strategies, and unbreakable team spirit.

The final whistle blew, and the St. Andrews girls had emerged victorious. They had defeated the reigning champions and won the regional tournament, a historic achievement that sent shockwaves through the world of girls' rugby.

As they stood on the field, holding the championship trophy aloft, Fiona couldn't help but reflect on their journey. They had started as underdogs, a newly formed team with a passion for rugby. But with the guidance of Coach Thompson and their unwavering dedication, they had become the 'unstoppable scrum,' a team that had risen to the top against all odds.

Their victory was not just about winning a tournament; it was about breaking barriers and proving that with hard work, determination, and the right guidance, even the most formidable opponents could be overcome.

The town of St. Andrews celebrated their girls' rugby team with pride and joy. The girls had not only brought home a championship but had also inspired a new generation of young players, both boys and girls, to take up the sport with passion and dedication.

Coach Thompson watched with a sense of fulfillment as her team celebrated their victory. She knew that their journey was far from over, and there were more challenges and triumphs awaiting them. But for now, they had achieved something extraordinary, and they had done it together, as an unbreakable team.

The story of the 'unstoppable scrum' became a source of inspiration not just in their town but throughout Scotland. It was a testament to the power of teamwork, determination, and the belief that even underdogs could achieve greatness.

As they celebrated their victory, the St. Andrews girls knew that their journey in rugby was just beginning. They had proven that they were a force to be reckoned with, and they were ready to face whatever challenges lay ahead with the same unwavering spirit and determination that had brought them this far.

Part 5

The victory in the regional tournament had been a monumental achievement for the St. Andrews Primary School girls' rugby team, known throughout their town as the 'unstoppable scrum.' Their triumph over the reigning champions had sent shockwaves through the world of girls' rugby in Scotland.

As they stood on the field, holding the championship trophy aloft, Fiona, their determined captain, couldn't help but feel a sense of pride and accomplishment. Their journey had been nothing short of extraordinary, a testament to their hard work, clever strategies, and unwavering team spirit.

The town of St. Andrews celebrated their girls' rugby team with fervor and joy. The girls had not only brought home a championship but had also inspired a new generation of young players, both boys and girls, to take up the sport with passion and dedication.

Coach Thompson watched with satisfaction as her team celebrated their victory. She knew that their journey was far from over, and there were more challenges and triumphs awaiting them. But for now, they had achieved something extraordinary, and they had done it together, as an unbreakable team.

The victory in the regional tournament had earned them recognition not just in their town but throughout Scotland. They were now seen as a formidable force in girls' rugby, a team that had risen to the top against all odds. Their story became a source of inspiration for aspiring young players, a reminder that with hard work, determination, and the right guidance, even the most formidable opponents could be overcome.

With their heads held high, the St. Andrews girls returned to their school, greeted by cheering classmates, teachers, and proud parents. They had not only made history but had also shattered the stereotypes and barriers that had once held them back.

As they resumed their regular training sessions, the girls knew that they couldn't rest on their laurels. Their next challenge loomed on the horizon – the national tournament, where they would face the top teams from all over Scotland.

The national tournament was the pinnacle of girls' rugby in Scotland, a competition that would test their skills, strategies, and teamwork like never before. It was a chance to prove that their victory in the regional tournament was not a fluke but a testament to their true potential.

Coach Thompson wasted no time in preparing her team for the national tournament. She introduced new drills and tactics, pushing the girls to refine their skills and expand their knowledge of the game. She reminded them that they were no longer underdogs; they were contenders, and they needed to approach every match with confidence and determination.

The weeks leading up to the national tournament were filled with intense training sessions, video analysis, and discussions about their opponents' playing styles. The St. Andrews girls were no longer just passionate players; they were students of the game, constantly seeking ways to improve and outsmart their opponents.

Fiona, in her role as captain, took on the responsibility of motivating her teammates and keeping their spirits high. She knew that the national tournament would be a daunting challenge, but she believed in their abilities and in the lessons they had learned from Coach Thompson.

The day of the national tournament arrived, and the St. Andrews girls traveled to the venue with a mixture of excitement and nerves. The competition was fierce, with teams from all over Scotland gathered for the prestigious event.

Coach Thompson gathered the team for a final pep talk before their first match. "This is the moment we've been working towards," she said. "You've proven that you belong here, and now it's time to show the world what you're capable of. Remember everything we've learned – teamwork, strategy, and the belief in yourselves."

The girls nodded in agreement, their determination shining through. They knew that they had the skills and the mindset to compete at the highest level.

Their first match in the national tournament was against a team that had a reputation for relentless defense and powerful forwards. It was a tough challenge, but the St. Andrews girls were ready.

From the kickoff, it was clear that this would be a closely contested match. The opposing team's defense was formidable, and their forwards were relentless in their tackles.

The St. Andrews girls employed the strategies and tactics they had learned from Coach Thompson. Their passes were precise, and they moved the ball swiftly to create scoring opportunities. Fiona's ability to read the game was evident as she orchestrated plays that tested the opposing defense.

As the match progressed, the St. Andrews girls found themselves trailing by a narrow margin. The tension on the field was palpable, and the crowd watched with bated breath.

In a pivotal moment, Fiona made a quick decision during a scrum. She signaled to her teammates, and they executed the play flawlessly. The opposing team was caught off guard, and the St. Andrews girls seized the opportunity.

With a burst of speed and a perfectly timed pass, they moved the ball swiftly down the field. Fiona, with determination in her eyes, sprinted toward the try line. She could hear the cheers of her teammates, the roar of the crowd, and the pounding of her heart in her chest.

As she reached the try line, Fiona made a split-second decision. Instead of attempting to score the try herself, she passed the ball to her teammate, Sarah, who was in a better position to cross the line. Sarah seized the opportunity and dove over the try line, scoring the winning try.

The crowd erupted in cheers, and the St. Andrews girls rushed to embrace Fiona and Sarah. It was a hard-fought victory, a testament to their determination and clever play.

Their first match in the national tournament had set the tone for the rest of their journey. The St. Andrews girls continued to excel, winning match after match with their clever strategies, precise execution, and unwavering teamwork.

As they advanced through the tournament rounds, their confidence grew. They faced formidable opponents, but they were no longer underdogs; they were contenders, and they played like champions.

In the semifinals, they faced a team that had been dominant in girls' rugby for years. It was a clash of titans, a match that would test their skills and determination to the fullest.

The match was a fierce battle, with both teams displaying their best rugby. The St. Andrews girls played with heart and determination, executing their strategies with precision.

As the final whistle blew, the scoreboard showed a narrow victory for the St. Andrews girls. It was a stunning upset, and their jubilant celebration echoed through the tournament venue.

They had advanced to the finals of the national tournament, a chance to prove that their victory in the regional tournament was not a fluke but a testament to their true potential.

The finals of the national tournament were a grand spectacle, with a large crowd in attendance. The St. Andrews girls faced a team that had won the tournament for several years running, a team known for their skill, speed, and tactical brilliance.

The odds were stacked against the St. Andrews girls, but they were undeterred. They had come this far, and they believed in their abilities and in the lessons they had learned from Coach Thompson.

The final match was a breathtaking display of rugby prowess. Both teams played with precision and determination, each try and tackle met with thunderous applause from the crowd.

As the game entered its final moments, the score was tied. The tension on the field was palpable, and the crowd watched with bated breath. It was a moment that would define the St.

Andrews girls' journey – a chance to prove that with teamwork and smart play, even underdogs could rise to the top.

In a heart-pounding sequence of plays, the St. Andrews girls found themselves in possession of the ball. The opposing team's defenders closed in, their tackles relentless. Fiona knew that she had to make a decision, and she had to make it quickly.

With a burst of speed and a strategic sidestep, Fiona evaded the defenders and sprinted toward the try line. She could hear the roar of the crowd, the cheers of her teammates, and the pounding of her heart in her chest.

As she reached the try line, Fiona made a split-second decision. Instead of attempting to score the try herself, she passed the ball to her teammate, Emma, who was in a better position to cross the line. Emma seized the opportunity and dove over the try line, scoring the winning try.

The crowd erupted in cheers, and the St. Andrews girls rushed to embrace Fiona and Emma. It was a moment of triumph, a culmination of months of hard work, determination, and unwavering teamwork.

The final whistle blew, and the St. Andrews girls had emerged victorious. They had defeated the reigning champions and won the national tournament, a historic achievement that sent shockwaves through the world of girls' rugby in Scotland.

As they stood on the field, holding the championship trophy aloft, Fiona couldn't help but reflect on their journey. They had started as underdogs, a newly formed team with a passion for rugby. But with the guidance of Coach Thompson and their unwavering dedication, they had become champions, a team that had risen to the top against all odds.

Their victory was not just about winning a tournament; it was about breaking barriers and proving that with hard work, determination, and the right guidance, even the most formidable opponents could be overcome.

The town of St. Andrews celebrated their girls' rugby team with pride and joy. The girls had not only brought home a championship but had also inspired a new generation of young players, both boys and girls, to take up the sport with passion and dedication.

Coach Thompson watched with a sense of fulfillment as her team celebrated their victory. She knew that their journey was far from over, and there were more challenges and triumphs awaiting them. But for now, they had achieved something extraordinary, and they had done it together, as an unbreakable team.

The story of the 'unstoppable scrum' became a source of inspiration not just in their town but throughout Scotland. It was a testament to the power of teamwork, determination, and the belief that even underdogs could achieve greatness.

Part 6

The final whistle had blown, and the St. Andrews Primary School girls' rugby team had emerged victorious in the national tournament, a historic achievement that had sent shockwaves through the world of girls' rugby in Scotland.

As the girls stood on the field, holding the championship trophy aloft, the crowd erupted in cheers. Parents, classmates, and rugby enthusiasts from all over the town had gathered to witness their triumph. It was a moment of pure joy and pride for the entire community.

Fiona, their dedicated captain, held the trophy high, a smile of satisfaction on her face. She looked around at her teammates, who were celebrating with unbridled enthusiasm. They had come a long way from being a newly formed team with a passion for rugby to becoming champions, a team that had risen to the top against all odds.

Coach Thompson stood on the sidelines, watching with a sense of fulfillment. She had been their guiding light, the driving force behind their transformation into a formidable team. Seeing her players achieve such a remarkable feat was a source of immense pride.

The town of St. Andrews celebrated their girls' rugby team with fervor and joy. Banners and posters adorned the streets, and a parade was organized in their honor. The girls rode through the town on a float, waving to the cheering crowd and proudly displaying their championship trophy.

Their victory had not only brought home a championship but had also shattered the stereotypes and barriers that had once held them back. Boys and girls of all ages were inspired to take up rugby, and the local rugby club saw a surge in new members.

The St. Andrews girls became local heroes, their story a source of inspiration for aspiring young players. They were invited to schools to share their journey and encourage others to pursue their dreams with dedication and passion.

Fiona, in particular, was hailed as a role model for young athletes. She received messages and letters from girls all over Scotland, thanking her for showing them that they could achieve greatness in the world of sports. Fiona humbly accepted the praise but remained grounded, knowing that their success was the result of teamwork and unwavering determination.

As the celebrations continued, the St. Andrews girls knew that their journey in rugby was far from over. They had proven themselves as a force to be reckoned with, and they were eager to face new challenges on the rugby field.

Coach Thompson gathered the team for a post-tournament reflection. "You've achieved something incredible," she began, her voice filled with pride. "But remember, this is just the beginning. There will be more challenges and triumphs ahead. What's important is that you never lose the spirit of teamwork and determination that got you here."

The girls nodded in agreement, their commitment to the sport unwavering. They knew that the road ahead would be filled with tough opponents and demanding matches, but they were ready to face them head-on.

Over the following months, the St. Andrews girls continued to train diligently. They refined their skills, honed their strategies, and worked on their fitness. Coach Thompson introduced new drills and tactics, pushing them to become even better players.

Their success in the national tournament had earned them recognition not just in Scotland but throughout the UK. They were invited to participate in regional and national competitions, where they faced teams from different parts of the country.

The St. Andrews girls welcomed the opportunity to compete at a higher level. They knew that the competition would be fierce, but they were determined to prove that their victory in the national tournament was not a fluke but a testament to their true potential.

Their matches against other regional and national teams were intense and challenging. The St. Andrews girls faced opponents with different playing styles and strategies, forcing them to adapt and innovate.

Fiona, as captain, continued to lead by example. Her ability to read the game and make split-second decisions had become a valuable asset for the team. She was not just a skilled player but also a mentor to her teammates, always encouraging them to push their limits.

The St. Andrews girls also learned the importance of resilience in the face of defeat. They faced losses and setbacks, but they never allowed them to deter their spirits. Coach Thompson reminded them that every defeat was an opportunity to learn and grow as players.

As they continued to compete in regional and national competitions, the St. Andrews girls gained a reputation for their clever strategies, precise execution, and unwavering teamwork. They were no longer just a local sensation; they were a force to be reckoned with on the national stage.

Their journey in rugby took them to various parts of the UK, and they formed friendships with players from different teams. They shared their stories of determination and success, inspiring others to pursue their passions with dedication.

One of the most memorable moments of their journey was a friendly match against a team from Wales. The St. Andrews girls traveled to Wales, where they were welcomed with warmth and camaraderie.

The match was a thrilling display of rugby prowess, with both teams giving their all on the field. In the end, the St. Andrews girls emerged victorious, but the true victory was the bond of friendship that they had formed with their Welsh counterparts.

As the years went by, the St. Andrews girls continued to excel in rugby. Some of them received scholarships to prestigious rugby academies, while others pursued higher education with the sport as a central part of their lives.

Fiona, true to her passion for rugby, went on to represent Scotland in international tournaments. She became a symbol of excellence in the sport, a player whose journey had inspired a generation of young athletes.

Coach Thompson, too, continued to mentor and guide young players, passing on her knowledge and experience. She took pride in the success of her former team, knowing that they had become not just skilled rugby players but also strong, resilient individuals.

The story of the 'unstoppable scrum' became a legendary tale in the world of girls' rugby. It was a testament to the power of teamwork, determination, and the belief that even underdogs could achieve greatness.

The town of St. Andrews continued to support their girls' rugby team with unwavering enthusiasm. The girls had not only brought home a championship but had also brought the community together, fostering a sense of pride and unity.

The legacy of the 'unstoppable scrum' lived on, inspiring generations of young players to take up rugby and pursue their dreams with dedication and passion. The girls had not only achieved greatness on the rugby field but had also left an indelible mark on the hearts and minds of those who had witnessed their remarkable journey.

As they looked back on their journey, the St. Andrews girls knew that they had achieved something extraordinary. They had started as underdogs, a newly formed team with a passion for rugby, and had risen to become champions, a team that had defied the odds and proven that with hard work, determination, and the right guidance, even the most formidable opponents could be overcome.

Their story was a shining example of the power of teamwork and the indomitable spirit of youth. It was a testament to the belief that, with unwavering determination, anyone could achieve greatness and leave a lasting legacy for generations to come.

And so, the 'unstoppable scrum' continued their journey, their spirits unbroken, their determination unwavering, and their hearts filled with the love of rugby. They knew that no matter what challenges lay ahead, they would face them together, as an unbreakable team, ready to conquer new heights and make their mark on the world of rugby once again.

The End.

The International Exchange

Part 1

The sun hung low in the sky as twelve-year-old Sophie sat on her bedroom floor, her rugby ball beside her. She had been practicing her passes, kicks, and tackles for hours, and now she was taking a moment to catch her breath. Sophie was a skilled rugby player, and she loved the sport more than anything else in the world.

Living in a small town in England, rugby was more than just a game; it was a way of life. Sophie's family had a rich history of rugby players, and she was determined to carry on the tradition. Her room was adorned with posters of her rugby heroes, and her shelves were filled with books about the sport.

Sophie's passion for rugby had not gone unnoticed. She was the star player of her school's girls' rugby team, known for her agility, speed, and strategic thinking on the field. But on this particular evening, something extraordinary was about to happen.

Sophie's mother knocked on the door and entered with a wide smile. "Sophie, you'll never believe what I just received in the mail," she said, holding an envelope.

Sophie looked up, her curiosity piqued. "What is it, Mum?"

With a flourish, her mother opened the envelope and pulled out a letter. She began to read it aloud, her voice filled with excitement. "Dear Sophie, we are thrilled to inform you that you have been selected for the international rugby exchange program. You will have the opportunity to spend a month in New Zealand, a country renowned for its rugby heritage. There, you will train and play with a local girls' rugby team. This is a prestigious opportunity, and we believe it will be an enriching experience for you both as a player and as an individual."

Sophie's eyes widened as she listened to the words. An international rugby exchange program? New Zealand? It was a dream come true for any rugby enthusiast, and Sophie couldn't believe her luck.

Her mother continued, "You were chosen because of your dedication and skill on the field. We are so proud of you, darling."

Sophie's heart swelled with pride and excitement. She had always dreamed of taking her rugby skills to new heights, and now she had the chance to do just that. But there was one question burning in her mind. "When do I leave, Mum?"

Her mother smiled warmly. "You'll be flying to New Zealand in two weeks. You have some time to prepare and say your goodbyes."

Two weeks felt both like an eternity and a blink of an eye to Sophie. She could hardly contain her excitement as she thought about the adventures that awaited her in the land of rugby legends.

As the days passed, Sophie threw herself into rigorous training. She wanted to be in the best possible shape when she arrived in New Zealand. She practiced her passes with her father, honed her kicking accuracy, and ran laps around the local park to improve her speed and endurance.

Her friends from the school rugby team gathered to give her a heartfelt send-off. They presented her with a rugby ball signed by the entire team and wished her luck on her journey. Sophie promised to bring back new skills and stories to share with them.

With each passing day, Sophie's excitement grew, but so did her nervousness. She had never been away from her family for such a long period, and the thought of being in a foreign country, even one as rugby-crazy as New Zealand, made her a little anxious.

On the eve of her departure, Sophie lay in bed, her mind buzzing with a mix of emotions. Her mother came into her room and sat down beside her. "Feeling nervous, love?" she asked gently.

Sophie nodded, unable to hide her apprehension. "A bit, Mum. What if I don't fit in or can't keep up with their training?"

Her mother brushed a strand of hair away from her face. "Sophie, you've worked hard to get where you are. You're a talented player, and this is a fantastic opportunity for you to learn and grow. Don't worry about fitting in; just be yourself, and everything will fall into place."

Sophie found comfort in her mother's words. She knew that she had the support of her family, friends, and teammates back home. With a determined smile, she whispered, "I'll make the most of this, Mum. I promise."

The next morning, Sophie's family drove her to the airport, where her adventure would begin. She clutched her passport and her rugby ball, feeling a mix of excitement and nervousness. As she said her goodbyes, her younger brother handed her a small teddy bear wearing a rugby jersey.

"Take this with you, Sophie," he said, his eyes filled with sincerity. "So you'll always have a piece of home with you."

Tears welled up in Sophie's eyes as she hugged her brother tightly. "Thank you, Jamie. I'll miss you all so much."

Her family waved her off as she walked through the airport gates, her heart filled with anticipation. The journey ahead was unknown, but Sophie was ready to embrace it with open arms.

She was on her way to New Zealand, the land of rugby legends, and she couldn't wait to discover what awaited her on the other side of the world.

Part 2

The flight to New Zealand felt like an eternity for Sophie. She had never been on a plane for such a long journey, and the excitement that had filled her when she boarded had gradually given way to a restless anticipation. She fidgeted in her seat, unable to sit still as she watched the hours tick by on the in-flight entertainment screen.

Finally, after what seemed like an eternity, the plane began its descent into Auckland, New Zealand. Sophie peered out of the window, her heart racing with a mix of nerves and excitement. As the plane touched down, she could hardly believe that she was on the other side of the world.

Once she had cleared customs and collected her luggage, Sophie stepped into the arrivals area of Auckland International Airport. She scanned the crowd, searching for a sign with her name on it. Just as she was beginning to worry, she spotted a friendly-looking woman holding a placard that read, "Welcome, Sophie!"

Sophie approached the woman, who had a warm smile on her face. "Hello, Sophie," she greeted. "I'm Mrs. Taylor, and we're so excited to have you here in New Zealand. My daughter, Maia, is eager to meet you."

Sophie felt an immediate sense of relief as Mrs. Taylor's welcoming demeanor put her at ease. "Thank you, Mrs. Taylor. I'm really excited to be here."

With Sophie's bags in tow, they made their way to the Taylors' car, where Mr. Taylor and Maia were waiting. Maia was around Sophie's age, with long brown hair and a confident air about her. She extended her hand with a grin. "Hi, Sophie! I've been looking forward to meeting you."

Sophie shook Maia's hand, feeling an instant connection. "Likewise, Maia. I can't wait to train and play rugby with you."

The Taylors' home was cozy and welcoming, and they went out of their way to make Sophie feel comfortable. As they sat down for dinner that evening, Sophie couldn't help but feel a pang of homesickness. She missed her family, her friends, and the familiar surroundings of her small English town.

Mrs. Taylor noticed Sophie's subdued mood and offered a reassuring smile. "It's natural to feel a bit homesick when you're far away from home, Sophie. But I promise, you'll settle in and start enjoying your time here in no time."

Maia chimed in, "And we're here to help you every step of the way. Tomorrow, I'll take you to meet the rest of the rugby team, and you'll see how friendly and welcoming they are."

Over the next few days, Sophie began her rugby training with the local girls' team. She quickly realized that rugby in New Zealand was different from what she was used to back in England. The training was intense, and the girls were incredibly skilled. Sophie felt like she was starting from scratch as she tried to keep up with their pace and precision.

One sunny afternoon, as the girls practiced their tackles and passes, Sophie's frustration bubbled to the surface. She couldn't help but feel inadequate compared to her New Zealand teammates. She missed her old team and the familiar drills they used to do.

Maia noticed Sophie's frustration and approached her during a water break. "You're doing great, Sophie. I know it's tough, but you'll get the hang of it. Our training here is more intense, but it'll make you a better player."

Sophie appreciated Maia's encouragement but couldn't shake off the feeling of being out of her depth. She confided in Maia, "I just miss my old team and the way we used to play. I feel like I don't belong here."

Maia placed a comforting hand on Sophie's shoulder. "I know it's hard, but remember why you're here. You wanted to challenge yourself and learn new skills. You're not here to be the best player right away; you're here to grow and improve."

Sophie nodded, taking Maia's words to heart. She knew that if she wanted to make the most of her time in New Zealand, she had to embrace the challenges and push herself to become a better rugby player.

As the days turned into weeks, Sophie's determination to improve began to pay off. She started to adapt to the faster pace of the game and the new techniques she was learning. Her teammates noticed her dedication and began to include her more in their drills and strategies.

Off the field, Sophie was becoming a part of the Taylor family. They took her on outings to explore New Zealand's stunning landscapes, from lush forests to picturesque beaches. One weekend, they visited a traditional Maori cultural event, where Sophie had the opportunity to learn about the indigenous culture of the country.

At the event, they watched powerful Maori haka performances, sampled delicious Maori cuisine, and even tried their hand at some traditional Maori games. Sophie was fascinated by the rich history and heritage of the Maori people, and she couldn't help but admire the deep connection between rugby and Maori culture.

One evening, as they sat around the dinner table, Mr. Taylor shared a story about the significance of rugby in New Zealand. "Rugby is more than just a sport here, Sophie. It's a part of our identity. It brings communities together, and it's a source of pride for all New Zealanders."

Mrs. Taylor added, "The All Blacks, our national rugby team, are like national heroes. They inspire young players like you to aim high and dream big."

Sophie listened intently, realizing that rugby in New Zealand went beyond the field; it was a part of the country's soul. She felt honored to be a part of it, even if only for a short time.

With each passing day, Sophie grew more accustomed to her new surroundings and the different style of rugby she was learning. She became good friends with her teammates, who not only helped her on the field but also introduced her to the local culture and traditions.

One bright morning, as they gathered for another intense training session, Sophie felt a newfound sense of confidence. She was no longer the hesitant newcomer but a determined player eager to contribute to her team.

Part 3

As Sophie continued her rugby training in New Zealand, she found herself faced with a daily dose of challenges and new experiences. The girls on the local team, known as the 'Kiwi Kickers,' were exceptionally talented, and their style of play was distinct from what Sophie had been accustomed to back in England.

One of the major differences Sophie noticed was the pace of the game. In New Zealand, rugby was played with lightning speed. The Kiwi Kickers moved the ball swiftly between players, executed complex plays with precision, and seemed to have an uncanny ability to read the game. Sophie, on the other hand, often found herself struggling to keep up.

One sunny afternoon, after a particularly intense training session, Sophie sat down on the grass, sweat trickling down her forehead. Maia, always supportive, sat beside her. "You're doing really well, Sophie," Maia said with a reassuring smile. "I can see that you're improving every day."

Sophie nodded but couldn't shake off the frustration that had been building within her. "I know, Maia, but I still feel like I'm not at the same level as the rest of the team. They're so fast and skilled, and sometimes I feel like I'm holding them back."

Maia placed a comforting hand on Sophie's shoulder. "I understand how you feel, but remember, you're here to learn and grow. It's normal to face challenges when you're trying something new. The important thing is that you're putting in the effort, and that's what matters most."

Sophie appreciated Maia's encouragement, but she couldn't help but wonder if she would ever truly fit in with the Kiwi Kickers. She longed for the familiarity of her old team and the comfort of playing in a style she had mastered over the years.

As the weeks passed, Sophie's determination to adapt to the New Zealand style of play only grew stronger. She spent hours practicing with Maia, working on her passing accuracy and speed. She watched videos of the Kiwi Kickers' matches, analyzing their strategies and trying to understand the nuances of their game.

One evening, as they practiced passing on the beach, Maia offered some valuable advice. "You know, Sophie, rugby is not just about being the fastest or the strongest. It's about strategy and teamwork. In New Zealand, we emphasize playing as a cohesive unit. If we work together effectively, we can outsmart even the fastest opponents."

Sophie nodded thoughtfully. She had always been a strategic player back home, and perhaps that was a quality she could bring to the Kiwi Kickers. "You're right, Maia. I need to focus on playing smart and working as part of the team."

With Maia's guidance, Sophie began to shift her perspective. Instead of trying to match the Kiwi Kickers in speed and agility, she focused on her ability to read the game and make strategic decisions. During drills, she would position herself strategically, anticipating the movements of her teammates and opponents.

As Sophie's understanding of the game deepened, her performance on the field started to improve. She became known for her keen sense of strategy and her ability to set up scoring opportunities for her teammates. The Kiwi Kickers began to appreciate her unique contributions to the team.

Off the field, Sophie was fully embracing the New Zealand way of life. She had grown close to the Taylor family, who had become like a second family to her. They often spent weekends exploring the beautiful landscapes of New Zealand, from hiking in lush forests to surfing on pristine beaches.

One weekend, they ventured into the countryside, where Sophie experienced the awe-inspiring beauty of New Zealand's natural wonders. They visited towering waterfalls, hiked through dense rainforests, and marveled at the crystal-clear lakes. Sophie couldn't help but feel a deep connection to the land, and she was grateful for the opportunity to explore such breathtaking landscapes.

One evening, as they sat around a campfire under a starlit sky, Mr. Taylor shared stories about New Zealand's rugby legends and their deep connection to the land. "Rugby in New Zealand isn't just a sport; it's a way of life. The love for the game is passed down through generations, and it's deeply intertwined with our culture and the land we call home."

Mrs. Taylor added, "Playing rugby here is not just about winning; it's about playing with heart and soul, giving it your all, and respecting your teammates and opponents. It's a lesson that goes beyond the field."

Sophie listened intently, realizing that rugby in New Zealand was more than just a game; it was a profound cultural experience. She felt privileged to be a part of it, even if only for a short time.

With each passing day, Sophie's bond with Maia grew stronger. They had become inseparable on and off the field, sharing not only their love for rugby but also their dreams and aspirations. Maia's friendship had been a lifeline for Sophie during her time in New Zealand, and she couldn't imagine her journey without her by her side.

One sunny afternoon, as Sophie and Maia practiced their kicking on the rugby pitch, Maia turned to her with a grin. "You know, Sophie, you've come a long way since you first arrived here. You're not just adapting to our style of play; you're excelling in it."

Sophie smiled, grateful for Maia's unwavering support. "I couldn't have done it without you, Maia. You've been an amazing friend and mentor."

As they continued their training, Sophie knew that she still had much to learn and improve upon, but she was determined to make the most of her time in New Zealand. She had embraced the challenges and differences, and she was becoming a true Kiwi Kicker, both in spirit and in skill.

Part 4

As Sophie continued her rugby journey in New Zealand, she found herself not only adapting to the style of play but also immersing herself in the rich culture of her newfound home. The Taylor family had made sure that she experienced the best of New Zealand's traditions, from its captivating landscapes to its deeply rooted customs.

One weekend, the Taylors took Sophie on a road trip to Rotorua, a region known for its geothermal wonders and Maori culture. Sophie was excited to explore this new facet of New Zealand and learn more about its indigenous people.

Their first stop was Te Puia, a Maori cultural center nestled in the heart of Rotorua. Sophie was immediately captivated by the powerful haka performance, a traditional Maori dance that conveyed strength and pride. The rhythmic chants and intimidating postures of the performers left a lasting impression on her.

After the performance, the Taylors introduced Sophie to a Maori guide who explained the significance of the haka. "The haka is a way for Maori to express their emotions, whether it's before battle, to welcome guests, or to celebrate achievements. It's a sacred tradition that has been passed down through generations."

Sophie was fascinated by the depth of Maori culture and its connection to rugby. She realized that the haka she had witnessed was not just a performance but a reflection of the passion and pride that New Zealanders had for their sport.

During their time in Rotorua, they also visited a traditional Maori marae, or meeting place, where Sophie had the opportunity to participate in a powhiri, a formal Maori welcome ceremony. She was greeted with the hongi, a traditional Maori greeting where noses are pressed together, symbolizing the exchange of breath and sharing of life.

As they sat in the wharenui, the meeting house, Sophie felt a sense of reverence for the Maori culture and its strong connection to the land and community. She realized that rugby in New Zealand wasn't just about playing a game; it was about honoring traditions and embracing the spirit of unity.

Back in Auckland, Sophie continued to explore the local culture. She and Maia often spent weekends visiting museums, art galleries, and historical sites. Sophie was particularly drawn to the Maori art and artifacts on display, and she was intrigued by the intricate carvings and symbolic designs that told stories of the past.

One sunny afternoon, as they strolled through a local art market, Sophie was captivated by a piece of Maori-inspired jewelry. She carefully selected a necklace with a pendant shaped like a koru, a spiral-shaped design representing new life, growth, and renewal. It was a reminder of her time in New Zealand and the personal growth she had experienced.

As Sophie embraced the culture, she also savored the flavors of New Zealand cuisine. She tried classic Kiwi dishes such as pavlova, fish and chips, and the iconic meat pie. Mrs. Taylor often cooked traditional Maori dishes like hangi, a method of cooking food underground using heated stones, and Sophie relished the opportunity to taste these unique flavors.

One evening, the Taylors invited Sophie to join them for a traditional Maori feast called a hākari. The meal featured an array of delicious dishes, including seafood, meats, and kumara, a sweet potato native to New Zealand. Sophie enjoyed every bite, savoring the flavors and the sense of community that came with the meal.

During dinner, Mr. Taylor shared stories of his own rugby experiences in New Zealand. "Rugby is a part of who we are as Kiwis," he said. "It's not just about winning; it's about the camaraderie, the teamwork, and the respect for one another. It's a sport that brings people together, and I'm glad you're getting to experience it firsthand, Sophie."

Sophie nodded, feeling grateful for the warmth and hospitality of the Taylors. She had not only grown as a rugby player but also as a person, gaining a deeper appreciation for the culture and values of New Zealand.

One weekend, the Taylors took Sophie on a special outing to the Auckland War Memorial Museum. It was a place where Sophie could learn about the country's history, including its involvement in both World Wars and the contributions of New Zealand soldiers.

As they walked through the museum, Sophie was struck by the stories of bravery and sacrifice. She read about the ANZACs (Australian and New Zealand Army Corps) and their shared history. Sophie couldn't help but draw parallels between the dedication of those soldiers and the commitment of rugby players, both willing to give their all for a greater cause.

After visiting the museum, they ventured to the nearby Auckland Domain, a large park surrounded by lush greenery. As they sat on the grass, Sophie reflected on her time in New Zealand. She had not only improved her rugby skills but had also gained a deeper understanding of the country's culture and the values that were integral to rugby.

Maia turned to Sophie with a grin. "You've experienced so much of New Zealand in such a short time, Sophie. I'm glad you've embraced our culture and traditions."

Sophie smiled warmly. "I wouldn't have wanted it any other way, Maia. This journey has been about more than just rugby. It's been about discovering a new world and the incredible people who call it home."

As the weeks turned into the final stretch of Sophie's stay in New Zealand, she felt a profound sense of gratitude. She had not only grown as a rugby player but had also developed a deep connection to the country and its culture. Sophie knew that these experiences would stay with her long after she returned to England.

With each passing day, Sophie was more determined than ever to make the most of her remaining time in New Zealand and continue to learn and grow, both on and off the rugby field.

Part 5

The day of the big match had arrived. It was a sunny Saturday afternoon, and the rugby field was buzzing with excitement. The Kiwi Kickers were facing off against a formidable local team, the Auckland Titans, in what was anticipated to be a thrilling showdown.

Sophie could feel the tension in the air as she and her teammates gathered in the locker room before the match. Coach Sarah, who had been tirelessly preparing them for this moment, gave a final pep talk. "Remember, girls, this is our chance to show what we've learned and how far we've come. Trust in each other, play as a team, and give it your all out there."

The Kiwi Kickers nodded in unison, their determination shining through. Sophie felt a mixture of nerves and excitement coursing through her. This was her opportunity to not only showcase her skills but also to contribute to the team's success.

As they stepped onto the field, Sophie couldn't help but notice the size and strength of the Auckland Titans. They were an imposing opponent, known for their physicality and relentless style of play. It was clear that the Kiwi Kickers would face a formidable challenge.

The match kicked off, and from the very start, it was intense. The Titans displayed their aggressive style, quickly gaining possession of the ball and launching into powerful attacks. Sophie and her teammates were immediately put to the test as they defended their goal line.

Sophie found herself in the thick of the action, tackling opponents and working tirelessly to regain possession of the ball. She relied on the skills she had developed during her time in New Zealand, focusing on her strategic positioning and decision-making. It was clear that the Kiwi Kickers were playing as a cohesive unit, supporting each other and trusting in their abilities.

Despite the Titans' relentless attacks, the Kiwi Kickers held their ground, refusing to concede points easily. Sophie was impressed by the resilience and determination of her teammates. They were putting up a formidable defense, and it was clear that they had absorbed the lessons Coach Thompson had imparted.

As the first half drew to a close, Sophie couldn't help but feel a sense of pride. The score was still tied, and the Kiwi Kickers were proving that they could hold their own against a powerful opponent. Coach Sarah's halftime talk was filled with encouragement and praise for their efforts.

"We're playing a fantastic game, girls," she said. "We've shown that we can match their physicality and intensity. Now, let's focus on our game plan and execute it with precision. We have the skills and the teamwork to win this."

The second half began, and the Kiwi Kickers came out with renewed determination. They implemented their game plan, focusing on quick passes, strategic kicks, and teamwork. Sophie could feel the energy on the field as they worked together seamlessly.

As the minutes ticked away, the Titans continued to press forward, determined to break through the Kiwi Kickers' defense. Sophie knew that they needed a breakthrough moment, a chance to turn the tide of the match.

It was during a crucial scrum that Sophie saw an opportunity. The ball had been won by the Kiwi Kickers, and Sophie, who had been positioned as the scrum-half, saw a gap in the Titans' defense. With a quick pass, she delivered the ball to Maia, who was waiting on the wing.

Maia, with her lightning speed, sprinted down the sideline, leaving the Titans in her wake. The crowd erupted into cheers as Maia crossed the try line, scoring a magnificent try. It was a moment of pure brilliance, a testament to the Kiwi Kickers' teamwork and strategy.

The Kiwi Kickers now led the match, and the Titans were left stunned by the sudden turn of events. Sophie and her teammates celebrated Maia's try, knowing that it had been a collective effort. They had executed their game plan flawlessly, and it had paid off.

With only minutes left in the match, the Titans mounted one final assault. They pushed forward with all their might, determined to score and equalize. The Kiwi Kickers' defense held strong, and Sophie, with her strategic thinking, made crucial tackles to prevent the Titans from advancing.

As the final whistle blew, the Kiwi Kickers emerged victorious, with a score of 10-7. The crowd erupted into cheers, and Sophie and her teammates celebrated their hard-earned win. It was a moment of triumph, a culmination of weeks of dedication and growth.

The Titans, though disappointed by the loss, showed their respect by applauding the Kiwi Kickers' performance. The two teams exchanged handshakes and words of sportsmanship, acknowledging the intensity of the match.

Sophie couldn't help but feel a sense of fulfillment. She had not only adapted to the New Zealand style of play but had also contributed to her team's success. Her journey in New Zealand had been about more than just improving her rugby skills; it had been a journey of self-discovery and personal growth.

As they gathered for a post-match huddle, Coach Sarah spoke with pride. "Girls, you've shown what it means to play with heart and teamwork. You've embraced the New Zealand style of rugby, and today, you've proven that you can compete at the highest level. I couldn't be prouder of each one of you."

Sophie and her teammates exchanged smiles and hugs, knowing that this victory was a testament to their dedication and the lessons they had learned. Sophie had not only gained valuable rugby experience but had also formed deep bonds with her Kiwi Kicker family.

As they walked off the field, Sophie felt a sense of contentment. Her international exchange had been an unforgettable experience, filled with challenges, growth, and unforgettable moments. She knew that she would carry the lessons and memories of her time in New Zealand with her, not only as a rugby player but as a person enriched by the culture and values of a distant land.

Part 6

The weeks in New Zealand had passed by in a whirlwind of rugby matches, cultural experiences, and personal growth. As Sophie's time in Auckland came to a close, she found herself reflecting on the incredible journey she had embarked upon.

The day of her departure arrived, and Sophie stood at the Auckland International Airport with the Taylors by her side. The emotions were bittersweet as she prepared to bid farewell to the country that had become her second home.

Sophie turned to Maia, her closest friend and teammate in New Zealand. "I can't believe it's time to go, Maia. I'm going to miss you and everyone so much."

Maia hugged her tightly. "We'll miss you too, Sophie. You've been an amazing teammate and friend. Promise me you'll keep playing rugby when you're back in England."

Sophie smiled warmly. "I promise, Maia. I'll carry the lessons I've learned here with me and share them with my team in England. And who knows, maybe one day we'll meet on the rugby field again."

They exchanged heartfelt goodbyes, and Sophie boarded her flight, feeling a mix of sadness and gratitude. Her time in New Zealand had been a transformative experience, one that had expanded her horizons and enriched her life in ways she could never have imagined.

As the plane soared into the sky, Sophie looked out of the window, watching as the familiar landscape of Auckland grew smaller and smaller. She knew that this was not the end of her rugby journey but the beginning of a new chapter.

Back in England, Sophie was welcomed home with open arms by her family and friends. She couldn't wait to share her adventures and experiences with them. She had grown not only as a rugby player but as a person, and she wanted to inspire those around her with the lessons she had learned in New Zealand.

Her first stop was her rugby team's practice. She had missed her teammates dearly and was excited to reunite with them. Sophie walked onto the field with a newfound confidence and a deeper understanding of the sport.

Coach Thompson, who had been following Sophie's journey through emails and updates, was thrilled to see her back. "Welcome home, Sophie," she said with a warm smile. "I hear you've had quite the adventure in New Zealand."

Sophie nodded enthusiastically. "It was incredible, Coach. I've learned so much, and I can't wait to share it with the team."

Over the next few weeks, Sophie became a source of inspiration for her teammates. She introduced them to the strategies and techniques she had learned in New Zealand, emphasizing the importance of teamwork and adaptability. Her experiences had instilled in her a deep appreciation for the global rugby community and the diversity of playing styles.

One evening, as the sun dipped below the horizon during practice, Sophie shared a story with her teammates. "In New Zealand, rugby isn't just a sport; it's a way of life. It's about respecting traditions, embracing different styles of play, and always striving to improve. We may come from different parts of the world, but when we step onto the field, we're all united by our love for this game."

Her teammates listened intently, inspired by Sophie's words. They felt a renewed sense of purpose and dedication to their sport. Sophie had become a true leader on and off the field, embodying the spirit of rugby that transcended borders.

The highlight of Sophie's return was her first match with the team since coming back from New Zealand. Her family and friends gathered to cheer her on, eager to see how her international experience had shaped her as a player.

As the match began, Sophie felt a surge of excitement. She knew that this was her opportunity to put into practice everything she had learned. The opposing team was strong, but Sophie's team was well-prepared, thanks to her guidance.

The match was intense, with both teams displaying skill and determination. Sophie, now a key player for her team, showcased her strategic thinking, precise passes, and agile moves. Her teammates were quick to adapt to the strategies she had brought back from New Zealand.

In the closing minutes of the match, with the score tied, Sophie found herself in a familiar situation. The ball was in her hands, and the outcome of the game rested on her decision. Drawing upon the lessons she had learned in New Zealand, she made a split-second decision to pass to a teammate who was in a better position to score.

The move paid off, and her teammate crossed the try line, securing the victory. The crowd erupted into cheers, and Sophie's teammates surrounded her with gratitude and admiration. Sophie had not only scored points on the field but had also scored the hearts of her team and the spectators.

As Sophie walked off the field, her family rushed to congratulate her. Her parents beamed with pride, and her younger brother, James, looked up to her with newfound respect. Sophie had not only achieved success as a rugby player but had also become a role model for her family and friends.

In the weeks that followed, Sophie continued to excel in her rugby journey. She received an invitation to join a regional development squad, and her skills and leadership qualities were recognized by scouts and coaches.

However, for Sophie, the most rewarding aspect of her return was the impact she had on her community. She started volunteering to coach younger girls in her town who were interested in playing rugby. She shared stories of her international exchange and inspired them to pursue their passion for the sport.

One sunny afternoon, as she watched her young protégés practicing on the field, Sophie felt a sense of fulfillment. She knew that her journey had come full circle, from a small town in England to the rugby fields of New Zealand and back again. She had not only grown as a rugby player but had also become a catalyst for change in her community.

The story of Sophie's international exchange had a lasting impact, not only on her but on all those who had been a part of her journey. It was a testament to the power of sports to transcend borders, forge connections, and inspire individuals to reach their full potential.

As she looked up at the clear blue sky, Sophie couldn't help but smile. She had learned that the true essence of rugby lay not only in the game itself but in the values of respect, teamwork, and determination that it instilled in those who embraced it. Her international exchange had been a rugby adventure of a lifetime, and Sophie was ready for the countless adventures that awaited her on and off the field.

The End.

Thank-You Note From The Author

Dear Beloved Readers,

You've reached the final page of *Rugby Stories for Girls - Volume 1.*

Firstly, thank you so much for buying and reading my book. I hope you really enjoyed every page.

Writing really is my passion and I'd love to continue writing more fun books like this!

So, with this in mind, **it would be great if you could leave a review**.

Please do share your thoughts about this book. Not only do they allow me to keep writing, and competing with the big publishers, but I also read and enjoy every single review.

With boundless gratitude,

Tanya P. Lovejoy

Printed in Great Britain
by Amazon